Against Smoking

An Ottoman Manifesto

Aḥmad al-Rūmī al-Aqḥiṣārī
(d. 1041/1631 or 1043/1634)

Against Smoking

An Ottoman Manifesto

Introduction, Editio Princeps *and Translation*

by

YAHYA MICHOT

Foreword by

MOHAMMAD AKRAM NADWI

Interface Publications – Kube Publishing
1431/2010

بسم الله الرحمن الرحيم

COVER PHOTOGRAPHS
Front: Young smoker. Detail of a bowl, Turkey, 11th/17th c.
(Brussels, Musée du Cinquantenaire).
Back: Turkish coffee-house (J. Ludwigsohn, Constantinople, *c*. 1900).

Published in England by Kube Publishing Ltd. and Interface Publications Ltd.

Kube Publishing Ltd.
Markfield Conference Centre, Ratby Lane, Markfield
Leicestershire, LE67 9SY, United Kingdom
Tel: +44 (0) 1530 249230, Fax: +44 (0) 1530 249656
Website: www.kubepublishing.com
Email: info@kubepublishing.com

Interface Publications Ltd.
15 Rogers Street, Oxford, OX2 7JS, United Kingdom
Website: www.interfacepublications.com
Tel: +44 (0) 1865 510251
Email: secretary@interfacepublications.com

Distributed by Kube Publishing Ltd.

2nd impression 2010

ISBN: 978-1-84774-020-5 *casebound*

A Cataloguing-in-Publication data record for this book is available from the British Library.

Contents

Tobacco: a, flower; b, fruit

SOME eat a sort of opium called benghilik, *or* henebane, *which renders them more or less stupid and entertains them with the different visions that their mind, muddled by these vapours, presents to them; just as those who smoke tobacco may, in their melancholy, draw some satisfaction from the variety of clouds and figures that smoke creates in the air when it comes out of their pipes.*

Albertus Bobovius (ʻAlī Ufkī Bey), *Topkapi*, p. 136 (*c*. 1665)

List of Illustrations

"From the ceaseless smoking of the coffee-house riff-raff the coffee-houses were filled with blue smoke, to such a point that those who were in them could not see one another..." [1]

1 Ibrāhīm Peçevi (d. *c*. 1060/1650), quoted in B. Lewis, *Istanbul*, p. 134. Engraving from C. de Bruyn, *Voyages*, p. 431.

Foreword

I AM delighted to have been offered the opportunity to set down a few reflections about the theme of this book. The last time I heard Prof. Yahya Michot lecture in person, about a couple of years ago in Oxford, he was speaking about opium – a study he has since developed into the book *L'Opium et le Café* (Beirut–Paris: Albouraq, 2008). If this work on tobacco suggests that he is building an addiction to bad habits in the Muslim world, passed to and from the Europeans, it is not one that has affected his scholarly practice. Readers familiar with Michot's weighty monographs on Avicenna and Ibn Taymiyya will find here the same relentless curiosity, the same concern to know the history of the text, where it came from and where it went, to understand its information and argument and local cultural context, the same determination to present as literal a translation as is compatible with intelligible English, while recording the significant variations in the available manuscripts, the same copious and detailed notes on proper names and terms of art, a rich bibliography of relevant scholarly works, generous indexes, a long introduction which picks out what is interesting (and entertaining) for scholars of the period, with amusing asides on how similar a critique of smoking informs the ban newly enforced in modern Turkey, and numerous charming and delightful illustrations of the malodorous habit and its consequences. And all that is on top of the labour of love with which Michot began – personally locating and identifying al-Aqḥiṣārī's work in a bound volume of related manuscripts.

Smoking first came into the Muslim world in the 11th/17th century. The English introduced it to the Ottomans, and then it passed to India and the rest of the Muslim world. It was initially likened to the forbidden *muskirāt* and *mukhaddirāt*, substances that intoxicate or stupefy. Furthermore, it had a bad smell, something that the Prophet disliked, in particular at prayer time and other occasions of religious attention; it impacted the health; it established in some people the habit of self-indulgence with concomitant neglect of their religious, familial and social responsibilities. To spend money on it was thus to waste the wealth that God had provided to enable people to improve their lives. Aware of all these negatives associated with smoking, jurists naturally formed and expressed their opinions about it. However, they differed in the advice they gave, depending on the extent of their comprehension of the problems, and they failed to reach any consensus about it. One reason in particular for the disagreement was that it was something new and hence there could not have been any explicit text about it in the Qur'ān and Sunna and early legal writings. They resorted to analogy to infer a safe ruling; however, since they could not agree on the precise nature of the harm smoking entails for individuals and society, their analogical reasoning led them in different directions.

Initially, as I mentioned, most jurists likened tobacco to wine in sinfulness and harmfulness and accordingly considered it *ḥarām* (forbidden).[1] A number of the jurists from each of the four major Sunnī schools wrote treatises on it, the most famous being: *Naṣīḥat al-ikhwān fī shurb al-dukhān* by Ibrāhīm al-Laqānī, *Risāla fī taḥrīm al-dukhān* by al-Fakkūn, and *I'lām al-ikhwān bi-taḥrīm al-dukhān* by Ibn 'Allān. The rationale given in these works is more or less the same as that put forward by al-Aqḥiṣārī in the present epistle.

Then, as smoking became a general phenomenon, especially in some Sufi circles, another opinion appeared, not as popular as the first, but some important people adhered to it nevertheless. According to this opinion, smoking is *mubāḥ* (permissible).[2] Among the well known

1 Among the Ḥanafī jurists who subscribed to this view were al-Shurunbulālī, al-Musayyarī, al-Ḥaṣkafī, the author of *al-Durr al-Mukhtār*; among the Mālikīs, S. al-Sanhūrī, I. al-Laqānī, M. al-Fakkūn, Kh. b. A. al-Maghribī, A. b. Y. Ibn Ḥamdūn; among the Shāfi'īs, N. D. al-Ghazzī, al-Qalyūbī, M. 'A. Ibn 'Allān; among the Ḥanbalīs, A. al-Bahūtī and others. (See *al-Durr al-mukhtār* with *Ḥāshiyat* Ibn 'Ābidīn, vol. v, pp. 295–296; *Tahdhīb al-furūq* at the margin of *al-Furūq*, vol. i, pp. 216–217; *Fatḥ al-'Ālī al-Malik*, vol. i, pp. 118, 189–190; *Bughyat al-mustarshidīn*, p. 260; *Ḥāshiyat* al-Qalyūbī, vol. i, p. 69; *Ḥāshiyat al-jumal*, vol. i, p. 170; *Ḥāshiyat* al-Shirwānī on *Tuḥfat al-minhāj*, vol. iv, p. 237; *Maṭālib ūlī l-nuhā*, vol. vi, pp. 217–219; *al-Fawākih al-'adīda fī l-masā'il al-mufīda*, vol. ii, p. 78; al-Shawkānī, *Risālat irshād al-sā'il ilā dalā'il al-masā'il*, pp. 50-51).

2 Those who subscribed to this view were: among the Ḥanafīs, 'A. Gh. al-Nābulusī, al-Ḥaskafī, M. al-'Abbāsī al-Mahdī, the author of *al-Fatāwā l-mahdiyya*, Sh. D. al-Ḥamawī, the commentator on *al-Ashbāh wa l-naẓā'ir*; among the Mālikīs, 'A. al-

treatises composed in this vein are: ‘Abd al-Ghanī al-Nābulusī’s *al-Ṣulḥ bayn al-ikhwān fī ibāḥat shurb al-dukhān*, ‘Alī al-Ajhūrī’s *Ghāyat al-bayān li-ḥill shurb mā lā yughayyibu l-‘aql min al-dukhān*, ‘Abd al-Qādir al-Ṭabarī al-Makkī’s *Raf‘ al-ishtibāk ‘an tanāwul al-tunbāk*; and Mar‘ī ibn Yūsuf’s *al-Burhān fī sha’n shurb al-dukhān*. The argument of this group may be summarized in this way: smoking does not cause intoxication, does not lead to loss of intellect, does not cloud reasoning, and does not inflict any harm on the body; accordingly, its harmfulness being doubtful, it cannot be forbidden. To forbid it amounts to saying on behalf of God and His Messenger what God and His Messenger did not say. Thus, smoking tobacco continues to rest on the primordial ruling on things, namely that, if it is not known for certain that a thing is forbidden, then that thing is permissible.

Later still, by which time jurists had established the extent of the harmfulness and the nature of the evidence for that judgement in the sources, opinions settled on the middle position, namely that smoking is *makrūh* (disliked, reprehensible).[1] In fact the argument of this group is similar to the first group. The rather different judgement is perhaps owed to pragmatism. The earlier scholars, in their time, had issued the stronger verdict in hope of stopping smoking before it became a settled habit in the society and spread among the people. By the time of the

Ajhūrī and most later Mālikīs, like M. b. A. al-Dasūqī, A. b. M. al-Ṣāwī, M. al-Amīr and M. ‘A. Ibn Ḥusayn, the author of *Tahdhīb al-furūq*, followed him; among the Shāfi‘īs, al-Ḥafnī, al-Ḥalabī, A. b. ‘A. R. al-Rashīdī, al-Shabramallāsī, M. b. ‘A. D. al-Bābilī, ‘A. Q. al-Ṭabarī; among the Ḥanbalīs, M. b. Y. al-Karmī. Al-Shawkānī, a reformer of the Zaydī school, also holds the same view. (See *Ḥāshiyat* Ibn ‘Ābidīn, vol. v, pp. 295–296; *Tahdhīb*, vol. i, pp. 217–219; *Fatḥ*, vol. i, pp. 189–190; *Ḥāshiyat al-jumal*, vol. i, p. 170; *Ḥāshiyat* al-Shirwānī, vol. viii, p. 309; *Maṭālib*, vol. vi, p. 217; *al-Fawākih*, vol. ii, pp. 80–81; al-Shawkānī, *Irshād*, pp. 50-51; *al-Fatāwā l-mahdiyya*, vol. v, p. 298; al-Ḥamawī’s *Commentary* on *al-Ashbāh wa l-naẓā’ir*, vol. i, p. 98; *Ḥāshiyat* al-Dasūqī, vol. i, p. 50).

1 This view is held, among the Ḥanafīs, by Ibn ‘Ābidīn, Abū l-Su‘ūd and Mawlānā ‘A. Ḥ. al-Laknawī; among the Mālikīs, by Y. al-Ṣifatī; among the Shāfi‘īs, by ‘A. Ḥ. al-Shirwānī; among the Ḥanbalīs, by M. b. S. al-Ruḥaybānī, A. b. M. al-Manṣūr al-Tamīmī. (See *Ḥāshiyat* Ibn ‘Ābidīn, vol. v, p. 296; *Tahdhīb*, vol. i, p. 219; *Ḥāshiyat* al-Shirwānī, vol. iv, p. 237; *Maṭālib*, vol. vi, pp. 217–219; *al-Fawākih*, vol. ii, p. 80).

later scholars too many people were already addicted, so they lightened the wording and called it "disliked, reprehensible" in the hope that those more wary of risking offending God would keep or be drawn away from it. It is worth noting that among this group, the majority, especially in the Indian subcontinent and some parts of the Middle East, categorized tobacco smoking as *makrūh taḥrīmī* (disliked–forbidden). This is in fact a term from much earlier, traceable to Abū Ḥanīfa's student al-Shaybānī (d. 189/805?) who differentiated between two types of forbidden things: those which are expressly mentioned in the Qur'ān and Sunna and those which are made forbidden by analogical reasoning. For the former al-Shaybānī uses the term *ḥarām*, and for the latter he uses *makrūh*, making it clear that, for all practical purposes, the two are the same. The later jurists coined the expression *makrūh taḥrīmī* for those forbidden things which are not expressly mentioned in the Qur'ān and Sunna.

Al-Aqḥiṣārī's presentation of the argument in his epistle in the 11th/17th century remains as fresh and relevant today as it was then. The reasoning of the majority of today's jurists does not depart from his in any significant way. He pronounced smoking *ḥarām*; the jurists of today pronounce it as either *ḥarām* or *makrūh taḥrīmī* or *makrūh* but their supporting arguments remain much the same. Thus, Michot has discovered in al-Aqḥiṣārī's epistle a very valuable document of Ottoman times which demonstrates how Sunnī jurists dealt with this new problem. They clearly understood that this new habit was not just a personal choice issue; rather, it had serious implications for the ethos of the Islamic society of their time. They saw how the example of those afflicted by this addiction was sanctioning a new sort of behaviour in the society, where people were not literally drunk but resembled drunk people in their indolence about or negligence of religious and family responsibilities. In this respect, the document illustrates a central and distinguishing characteristic of Islamic ethics, namely that an individual's conduct sometimes needs to be weighed not only in the narrow, private circle of a single life but in the larger, public circle of what that individual's conduct enables or sanctions in the conduct of others in the same community.

The epistle is remarkable also for the way al-Aqḥiṣārī discusses the issue. His manner is orderly, methodical, coherent and balanced. He combines understanding of the theme and command of the Islamic sources he will use to derive a ruling, with an even, fair, objective temperament: thus, when presenting opinions contrary to his own, there is no display of anger or any use of wording that might hint at superiority or self-righteousness. Clearly, for him, the issue is not one of belonging to this or that faction or group; it is not about identity, but about honest, serious practice of the religion. Al-Aqḥiṣārī starts his discourse in scholarly style by distinguishing between futility (*ʻabath*), amusement (*laʻib*) and caprice (*lahw*). Then, besides religious arguments, he also advances some medical arguments, again sensibly and capably, which illustrates how, for jurists, Islamic rulings must take account of different aspects of the issue at hand and deal with them accordingly, from different angles and approaches. Michot comments: "Health considerations play a remarkable part in al-Aqḥiṣārī's argumentation. He uses medicine as a servant of jurisprudence, in order to demonstrate tobacco's harmfulness" (p. 26). Overall, the method of al-Aqḥiṣārī illustrates how jurists must make Islam responsive and relevant to the events of their time, consider their wider impact, and be sure of their own religious seriousness in offering a judgement, before they venture to consider that they have right to pass such a judgement.

Michot brings out in his Introduction some specific issues related to smoking, highly relevant to the daily life of a believer, and about which there is little disagreement among jurists. For example, all jurists agree that smoking is not allowed inside the mosque. Even those who hold the opinion of its permissibility forbid it inside mosques. They compare smoking tobacco with eating onions or garlic, the consumption of which, though permissible generally, is forbidden in the mosque on account of their odour which offends the angels and people attending the prayer. Similarly, a smoker whose mouth and breath retain the smell of smoking can be refused entry to a mosque. Indeed, many jurists consider other religious gatherings like the circles for teaching of the Qur'ān and *ḥadīth* in the same category as mosques. Ḥanafī and Mālikī jurists do not permit a smoker, who smells of his habit, to attend any such gathering; while Shāfiʻī jurists disapprove it. The jurists also disapprove a smoker leading the prayer; and they are unanimous that if someone smokes during the day while fasting, it breaks his fast. As for buying and selling tobacco, those jurists who forbid its consumption also forbid its production and trade in it.

We are indebted to Y. Michot for discovering and presenting this precious text, for editing it so thoroughly and for a conscientious English translation that will make it accessible to the widest possible readership. In his learned Introduction, Michot clears up the misunderstanding of some people who identified the author of this epistle with another Aqḥiṣārī, the famous Bosnian scholar Ḥasan Kāfī (d. 1024/1615). He also provides, for the first time in any European language, a useful biography of the author, and a good bibliography of his works, which, as Michot himself acknowledges, cannot be considered complete but suffices to indicate the range of al-Aqḥiṣārī's interests.

The book will appeal to teachers and students of Islam as a living tradition with strong continuities from its past. The topic of how smoking was viewed from an Islamic perspective in the $11^{th}/17^{th}$ century can serve as a point of entry for classroom discussions about similar issues today, which require a comparable balancing between reasonable private amusement or distraction and ingrained social habits that consistently entail wastage of time and neglect of committed attention to prayer and other religious duties – the examples that come to mind are television, mobile phones, and some forms of internet usage: these have the look of addictions in that there are tangible withdrawal symptoms. It does not follow that in these cases (unlike smoking) the harm outweighs the possible good, or that the difficulty of trying to forbid altogether is less than that of just trying to limit misuse informally. Those with more specialized interest in Islamic Legal issues in the Ottoman domains of the period, or in socio-economic history of commercial practices and their linkage with cultural attitudes, or in the migration of ideas and attitudes across the Islamic world – Michot hints at a fascinating "passage to India" of this text of al-Aqḥiṣārī – as well as those who are intrigued by manuscripts and the craft of establishing a good edition will find much in this book to instruct and delight them.

Mohammad Akram Nadwi

Oxford, 27 June 2009

Preface

CONTRARY to what is now claimed by dishonest or ignorant politicians opposed to its joining the EU, Turkey has for centuries been a major player on the European scene, culturally as much as politically. The Ottomans notably had a pivotal role in initiating "the West" not only to the delight of coffee drinking and the splendour of tulips, but also to the sensuous delirium of opium. For his reward, "the Turk" got literally "smoked"... According to the Egyptian Ibrāhīm al-Laqānī (d. 1041/1631), when the English, around 1600, by dissecting the corpse of a smoker, discovered that his heart had become "like a dry sponge, with big and small holes in it", they banned the tobacco imported from their colonies in the New World and "exported it to the countries of Islam". In the most amazing U-turn away from the teachings of a Prophet famous for his love of perfumes, the same Ottoman society which had elevated the creation and use of fragrances into one of the *Beaux-arts*, then succumbed, in just a few years, to the foul-smelling charm of the American poison. It would take centuries before lawmakers, in Turkey as well as in the EU or the US, impose warnings like "Tütün öldürüyor" or "Smoking kills" on cigarettes and other tobacco products. Various ulema realized the dangers of the new substance and addiction to it as soon as it spread amongst Muslims, but they were largely preaching in the wilderness, their forebodings and advice unheeded. This book presents the arguments of one of them and is dedicated to the noble memory of all his peers.

I now live and continue my academic pursuits in Hartford, the capital of Connecticut, a state famous for the high quality of the "wrapper" tobacco leaves it has been producing on an industrial scale for the last two centuries. My wife and I have just planted a *Nicotiana* in our front garden and, if it takes, will lovingly follow its growth over the next few months when, also, we will be able to enjoy the pleasure of walking between the flowering tobacco fields of the region. As for other direct experiences with the subject of this book, I am afraid there will be none since I do not smoke and my only – limited – expertise is of a philological nature. That being said, let it be known that I had great pleasure in exploring the world of Ottoman tobacco prohibitionists and it is this intellectual delectation which I hope to have been able to share with the reader.

I am grateful to the Director of the Süleymaniye Library for allowing me to examine Aḥmad al-Rūmī l-Aqḥisārī's manuscripts during my stay in Istanbul in May 2008 and providing me with various sets of photographs on CD-ROM. My hearty thanks are due to the learned signatory of the Foreword and dearest brother, Shaykh Mohammad Akram Nadwi. My gratitude also goes to Marion Nielsen, curator and caretaker at the Luddy/Taylor Connecticut Valley Tobacco Museum, who graciously welcomed me and taught me all I needed to know about tobacco farming. I am most indebted to Omama Diab, Mustapha Sheikh and Jamil Qureshi, with whom I discussed this book, who read drafts of it and suggested several improvements. It was a privilege to speak of my research on al-Aqḥisārī, Ottoman puritanism, tobacco, "and other pleasures" with the students at Hartford Seminary in March 2009 and I benefited greatly from their questions and comments.

Yahya M. Michot

Jumādā I 1430 – May 2009

Introduction

A FORGOTTEN PURITAN FROM ANATOLIA

BORN in Cyprus to a Christian family, Aḥmad al-Rūmī al-Aqḥiṣārī was taken away as a child after the Ottoman conquest of the island (977/1570–981/1573) and converted to Islam. He became a Ḥanafite *'ālim* and lived in Akhisar (western Anatolia), where he is said to be buried in the Uzun Taş cemetery. He seems to have spent only a short time in Istanbul. The date of his death is not known with certainty and he is misidentified by some authors as Ḥasan Kāfī Āqḥiṣārī (d. 1024/ 1615), the Bosniac scholar from Prusac. Al-Aqḥiṣārī's most famous work is *The Councils of the Pious – Majālis al-abrār*, a collection of one hundred religious reflections inspired by Prophetic traditions from *The Lamps of the Tradition – Maṣābīḥ al-Sunna* by the Afghānī Shāfi'ite traditionist and Qur'ān commentator Abū Muḥammad al-Ḥusayn al-Baghawī, also known as Ibn al-Farrā' (d. in Marw al-Rūdh, 516/ 1122?).[1]

Al-Aqḥiṣārī is sometimes said to have been a shaykh of the Sufi Khalwatiyya order, which was vehemently opposed by Qāḍīzādelis and criticised by Kātib Çelebi in *The Balance of Truth – Mīzān al-Ḥaqq*. Could this be due to another misidentification with some third Ḥasan, Rūmī or Āqḥiṣārī, about whom little is known and who really did belong to this important *ṭarīqa*? Perhaps. In any case, the milieu in which the author of the *Majālis* evolved was surely a very different one. First, like Ibn Taymiyya (d. 728/1328) and his disciple Ibn Qayyim al-Jawziyya (d. 751/1350), to whom he refers explicitly and whose texts he quotes extensively, he strongly condemns the veneration of tombs, in his *Refutation of the visitors of tombs – Radd al-Qabriyya* as well as in *Council XVII* of the *Majālis*.[2] Second, what al-Aqḥiṣārī writes in the

1 On al-Aqḥiṣārī, see Y. Michot, *Opium*, p. 54.

2 See al-Aqḥiṣārī, *Qabriyya*, MS. *Michot 0801*, f. 1v: "These are pages that I have selected from the *Ighāthat al-lahfān fī maṣā'id al-Shayṭān*, by the shaykh, the

first lines of his commentary (*sharḥ*) on *The Unique Pearl, concerning the Recitation of the Qur'ān – al-Durr al-yatīm fī l-tajwīd* by Birgivī Meḥmed Efendi (d. 981/1573) gives a clear indication of the high esteem in which he holds the spiritual father of Ottoman puritanism: "…the shaykh, the active and strong scholar (*al-'ālim al-'āmil al-qawī*) Meḥmed b. Pīr 'Alī al-Birgivī – may God make the Garden his refuge, give him to drink a pure beverage, and quench his thirst…"[1] Third, and more intriguing still, the relatively large number of ancient manuscripts in which the Turkish texts of Birgivī's *Waṣiyyet-Nāmeh*, the *Epistle – Risāleh* of Qāḍīzāde Meḥmed (d. 1045/1635)[2] and al-Aqḥiṣārī's *Creed – Risāleh fī l-'aqā'id* (or *Risāleh*, or *Waṣiyyet-Nāmeh*) are bound together in a sort of sacred trilogy leaves no doubt that, in the mind of many at the time, their religious views were both pivotal and convergent.[3] This means, in other words, that the supposedly Khalwatī author of the *Majālis* could well have been directly linked to, or even have played a seminal role in, the reformist movement, influenced by Ibn Taymiyya and Ibn Qayyim, which, during the Ottoman 10th/16th–11th/17th centuries, presages Wahhābism. Some twenty years ago, R. Peters remarked that "little is known about this tradition" of "Turkish fundamentalism" (or "revivalism"), adding that "it certainly deserves a

imām, the most learned, Ibn Qayyim al-Jawziyya – may God put his spirit with the spirits which have returned toward their Lord, satisfying Him and satisfied…"; *Majālis*, MS. *Michot 0402*, f. 50r: "Quoting his shaykh, Ibn Qayyim said in his *Ighātha* that this is the reason why the Lawgiver forbade adopting the tombs as places for prostration (*masājid*)…"

1 Al-Aqḥiṣārī, *Sharḥ*, MS. *Harput 429*, f. 1v. On Birgivī, see K. Kufrevī, *EI2*, art. *Birgewī*; S. Çavuşoğlu, *Movement*, pp. 48–59; A. Y. Ocak, *Oppositions*, p. 610; R. Peters, *Dervishes* (on an anti-Sufi riot started in Cairo, in 1123/1711, by Turkish students reading Birgivī).

2 On Qāḍīzāde and the Qāḍīzādelis, see S. Çavuşoğlu, *Movement*, and the references given in Y. Michot, *Opium*, p. 10, n. 4.

3 See for example the MS. *Michot 0802*, in which al-Aqḥiṣārī's *Risāleh* appears between those of Birgivī and Qāḍīzāde. Other manuscripts. joining these three writings are Istanbul, *Yazma Bağışlar 6494*; *Laleli 2461*, *2463*, *2468*, *2470*, *2473*, *2474*, *2476*, *2477*, *2478*, *2480*, *2481*, *2482*. Al-Aqḥiṣārī's *Creed* can also be found in MSS. Istanbul, *Haci Mahmud Efendi 1287*, ff. 159v–163r; *1291*, ff. 96r–110r; *Laleli* 2404, ff. 78v–84v.

closer study in order to find out how the essentially Ḥanbalite ideas of Ibn Taymiyya and Ibn Qayyim al-Jawziyya could survive in Ḥanafite Ottoman religious culture."[1] An exploration of the works of al-Aqḥiṣārī may provide part of the answer; hence my interest in him. Perhaps, moreover, one will eventually have to speak of those ideas as "thriving" rather than "surviving", at various moments of the history of Turkey.

The truth however remains that Aḥmad al-Rūmī al-Aqḥiṣārī is almost completely absent from modern studies of the Ottoman 10th/16th–11th/17th centuries.[2] This is also the case for the impact of his *Majālis*, before and after it was translated into Urdu,[3] on the genesis of contemporary Indian Islamic thought, be it Deobandi or Barelvi: it is still to be explored in detail. The fact that the *Majālis* is explicitly quoted, together with Ibn Taymiyya and Ibn Qayyim al-Jawziyya, in *al-Balāgh al-mubīn*, an anti-Hindu tract in Persian falsely attributed to Shāh Walī-ullāh Dihlawī (d. 1176/1762) but most probably written in India after 1831, nevertheless testifies to the centrality of its author and holds the promise of potentially surprising developments. In his study of *al-Balāgh al-mubīn*,[4] Marc Gaborieau acknowledges having "no further information" on al-Aqḥiṣārī's *Majālīs*. He does not therefore realize that this pre-Wahhābī Ottoman work of Ḥanafite puritanism, alongside reports of pilgrims coming back from Arabia and other forms of ideological "digestion" by Ibn ʻAbd al-Wahhāb or Muḥammad al-Shawkānī (d. 1250/1834), might have been an important channel through which reformist teachings, Taymiyyan and others, influenced

1 R. Peters, *Dervishes*, p. 109. On the "Ibn Taymiyya School" in Ottoman Turkey, see S. Çavuşoğlu, *Movement*, which is paving the way for a proper reassessment of the importance of this school; see also A. Y. Ocak, *Sciences*, pp. 263–265.

2 In *Movement* (p. 221), S. Çavuşoğlu mentions him briefly without realizing his importance for a study of Ottoman puritanical reformism. He is not mentioned in M. C. Zilfi, *Kadizadelis*, *Politics*. There is no article on al-Aqḥiṣārī in the *İslām Ansiklopedisi* published by the Türkiye Diyanet Vakfı.

3 Al-Aqḥiṣārī's *Majālis* was edited in Arabic, with interlinear translation into Urdu, first in Delhi in 1283/1866, and a second time in Lucknow, in 1321/1903; see Y. Michot, *Opium*, p. 51.

4 M. Gaborieau, *Tract*, pp. 220–221. I am grateful to M. Gaborieau for sending me a photocopy of *al-Balāgh al-mubīn*.

the pseudo-Walīullāhan text which he calls “an Indian “Wahhābī” tract” and, more generally, the so-called Indian “Wahhābism”.[1] Whatever its appeal might be, this hypothesis will of course need to be confirmed.

Indian avatars of al-Aqḥiṣārī’s Majālis[2]

There is no scholarly bibliography of Aḥmad al-Rūmī al-Aqḥiṣārī. Apart from the *Majālis*, his *Risāleh fī l-‘aqā’id*, his *Radd al-Qabriyya* and his commentary on Birgivī’s *al-Durr al-yatīm*, he authored several epistles that can be read in *majmū‘a*s like the MSS. Istanbul, *Darül-mesnevi 258*, *Harput 429*, *Kılıç Ali Paşa 1035*, *Reşid Efendi 985*, as well as in several other manuscripts. I established the following list of his Arabic epistles during a short period of research at the Süleymaniye Library in May 2008 and by consulting the manuscripts’ catalogue on

1 On Indian “Wahhābism” in the early 19th century and the controversy about its origins, as well as on Ibn Taymiyya’s influence in India during the 18th and 19th centuries, see M. Gaborieau, *Criticizing*, pp. 464–466.

2 Left: Title page of the edition and Urdu translation of the *Majālis*, *Khazīnat al-asrār*, Delhi, 1283/1866. Right: Title page of *al-Balāgh al-mubīn*, Lahore, reprint of 1962.

the *Yazmalar* website of the Turkish Ministry of Culture and Tourism.[1] It can't in any way be considered complete and its only purpose is to give some idea of the range of al-Aqḥiṣārī's interests:

1) *Ta'līqa 'alā tafsīr al-Qāḍī al-Bayḍāwī "La-hu mā fī al-samā' wa l-arḍ..." – Note on al-Qāḍī al-Bayḍāwī's exegesis of the Qur'ānic verse "To Him belongs what is in heaven and on the earth..."* MS. *Kasidecizade 736*, ff. 115v–125v.

2) *Sharḥ* al-Durr al-yatīm fī l-tajwīd – *Commentary on Birgivī's* Unique Pearl, concerning the Recitation of the Qur'ān. MSS. *Ali Emiri Arabi 53* (copied in 1083/1672), *4347*, ff. 13–43 (1066/1655); *Beyazit 189*; *Çelebi Abdullah Efendi 408*, ff. 67v–113v; *Harput 429*, ff. 1v–28r; *Ibrahim Efendi 29*, ff. 1v–54r; *Kılıç Ali Paşa 1035*, ff. 1v–30r; *Laleli 3094*, ff. 132v–189v; *Reşid Efendi 1008*, ff. 75v–95r; *Tırnovali 7*, ff. 36v–56v; *Yazma Bağışlar 1124*, ff. 1v–31v; *Yozgat 853*, ff. 167v–188v. Yazmalar: Amasya, *Beyazıt İ l Halk Kütüphanesi*, 05 Ba 1207/1, ff. 1v–49v (1161/1747); Ankara, *Adana İHK*, 01 Hk 192/1, ff. 1v–36r (1091/1679); 01 Hk 467/6, ff. 37v–70v; 01 Hk 816/4, ff. 37v–65 (1122/1709); *Afyon Gedik Ahmet Paşa İHK* , 03 Gedik 17581/4, ff. 171v–203r (1106/1693); *Çankırı İHK* , 18 Hk 389/3, ff. 101v–130r; *Eskişehir İHK* , 26 Hk 277/5, ff. 15v–55r; *Nevşehir Ürgüp Tahsin Ağa İHK*, 50 Ür 46/2, ff. 8v–47r (1135/ 1722); 50 Ür 181/4, ff. 51v–86r (1123/1710); 50 Ür 389 (1167/1753); *Ordu İHK*, 52 Hk 901/4 (1129/1716); Balıkesir, *İHK*,10 Hk 973/3, ff. 41v–68r (1144/1730); Çorum, *Hasan Paşa İHK* , 19 Hk 204/2, ff. 20v–43r (1135/1722); 19 Hk 3678/1, ff. 1v–56v; 19 Hk 3679/3, ff. 15v–51r; 19 Hk 3685/1, ff. 1v-30v; 19 Hk 3692/1, ff. 1v–37r (1078/1666); Diyarbakır, *İHK*, 21 Hk 252/6, ff. 119v–138v (1196/1781); Erzurum, *İHK*, 25 Hk 23892/1, ff. 1v–37v (1131/1718); Kastamonu, *İHK*, 37 Hk 334/9, ff. 231v–262v (1141/1727); 37 Hk 419/1, ff. 1v–37v; 37 Hk 475/4, ff. 96v–123r; Konya, *İHK*, 42 Kon 353/3, ff. 89v–106r (1165/1751); 42 Kon 1555/3, ff. 5v–31r; 42 Kon 4983/4, ff. 55v–80; 42 Kon 5687/2, ff. 28v–59r (1292/1875); *Gaziantep İHK* , 27 Hk

1 *www.yazmalar.gov.tr*. This wonderful e-catalogue of Turkey's manuscripts is in continuous progress. My survey ended on April 30th, 2009.

88/4, ff. 72v–104r (1083/1671); 27 Hk 93/11, ff. 148v–171r; *Isparta İHK*, 32 Hk 452/2, ff. 28v–59r (1292/1874); *Isparta Uluborlu İHK*, 32 Ulu 396/4, ff. 35v–80v; Manisa, *İHK*, 45 Hk 381/1, ff. 1v–55v; 45 Hk 948/1, ff. 1v–34v (1137/1723); 45 Hk 1656/3, ff. 64v–93r (1039/1629); 45 Hk 2937/9, ff. 82v–110v (1035/1625); 45 Hk 3599 (1130/1717); 45 Hk 4559/2, ff. 124v–163v (1180/1765); 45 Hk 6911/2, ff. 41v–72v; 45 Hk 8469; *Akhisar Zeynelzade Koleksiyon*, 45 Ak Ze 594/8, ff. 93v–132v (1148/1734); Trabzon, *İHK*, 61 Hk 321.

3) *Risāla fī l-radd ʻalā l-Ṣaghānī fī mawḍūʻāti-hi – Epistle refuting al-Ṣaghānī, concerning his invented traditions*. MS. *Darülmesnevi 258*, ff. 143r–147r.

4) *Risāla fī l-tawḥīd – Epistle on monotheism*. MSS. *Hafid Efendi 453*, ff. 116v–117v; *Harput 429*, ff. 118v–119v; *Kılıç Ali Paşa 1035*, ff. 68v–69r.

5) *Risāla fī anna l-nubuwwa afḍal mina l-wilāya – Epistle explaining that Prophethood is more eminent than Friendship* [*of God*]. MSS. *Harput 429*, ff. 38r–48r; *Reşid Efendi 985*, ff. 91r–95r.

6) *Risāla fī bayān marātib al-nafs wa marātib al-ʻibāda wa marātib al-tawḥīd – Epistle making clear the degrees of the soul, the degrees of worship, and the degrees of monotheism*. MSS. *Harput 429*, ff. 93v–100r; *Reşid Efendi 985*, ff. 110v–113v. Yazmalar: Manisa İHK, *Akhisar Zeynelzade Koleksiyon*, 45 Ak Ze 1602/11, ff. 116v–123r.

7) *Risāla fī dhikr al-lisān wa l-qalb – Epistle on the remembrance of God by the tongue and by the heart.*[1] MSS. *Darülmesnevi 258*, ff. 99v–104r; *Harput 429*, ff. 48v–54v; *Şehid Ali Paşa 1189*, ff. 88v–94r. See also a *Risāla fī l-dhikr – Epistle on the remembrance of God*, in MS. *Harput 429*, ff. 84v–93r. Yazmalar: Çorum, *Hasan Paşa İHK*, 19 Hk 797/4, ff. 8v–12r; Manisa, *İHK*, 45 Hk 2224/10, ff. 82r–93r; 45 Hk 2937/4, ff. 36v–42r.

[1] On the Ottoman controversies concerning the remembrance of God, see S. Çavuşoğlu, *Movement*, pp. 208–213.

8) *Risāla fī l-sulūk wa anna-hu lā budd li-l-sālik min murshid – Epistle on the wayfaring, and that the wayfarer must inevitably have a guide.* MS. *Harput 429*, ff. 73r–77v.

9) *Risāla fī l-taqlīd – Epistle on the imitation of an authority.*[1] MSS. *Darülmesnevi 258*, ff. 84v–91v; *Harput 429*, ff. 29r–37r; *Kılıç Ali Paşa 1035*, ff. 38v–48v. Yazmalar: Konya, *İHK*, 42 Kon 3824/12, ff. 38v–43v; *Isparta İHK*, 32 Hk 1484/9, ff. 38v–44v; Manisa, *İHK*, 45 Hk 2937/6, ff. 53v–62v.

10) *Risāla fī l-bid'at al-sayyi'a wa ghayr al-sayyi'a – Epistle on the innovation that is bad and that which is not bad.*[2] MSS. *Darülmesnevi 258*, ff. 104v–109v (1093/1682); *Harput 429*, ff. 158r–164v; *Reşid Efendi 985*, ff. 83r–86r.[3] Yazmalar: Manisa, *İHK*, 45 Hk 2937/2, ff. 21v–27r.

11) *Risāla fī dhamm al-bid'a – Epistle on the censure of innovation.* MS. *Harput 429*, ff. 54v–65r. Yazmalar: Manisa İHK, *Akhisar Zeynelzade Koleksiyon*, 45 Ak Ze 1602/10, ff. 106v–116v.

12) *Risāla fī bayān kull min ṣalāt al-raghā'ib wa ṣalāt al-barāt – Epistle making clear [the status of] the prayers of Raghā'ib and Berāt.*[4] MSS. *Darülmesnevi 258*, ff. 91v–99r; *Harput 429*, ff. 148r–157v; *Reisülküttab 1182*, ff. 123v–127r; *Reşid Efendi 985*, ff. 77v–83r. Yazmalar: Manisa, *İHK*, 45 Hk 2937/3, ff. 27v–36r.

13) *Risāla fī man' al-taṣliya wa l-tarḍiya wa l-ta'mīn waqta l-khuṭba – Epistle on the interdiction to ask for God's blessings on the Prophet and for His satisfaction with the Companions, as well as to say "Amen", during the Friday prayer's sermon.*[5] MSS. *Harput 429*,

[1] See Kātib Çelebi, *Keşf*, vol. i, col. 856.

[2] On the Ottoman controversies concerning good and bad innovations, see Kātib Çelebi, *Mīzān*, trans. Lewis, *Balance*, pp. 89–91; S. Çavuşoğlu, *Movement*, pp. 260–266; A. Y. Ocak, *Oppositions*.

[3] A marginal note, f. 83r, attributes this text to "Rūmī, author of the *Majālis*, and disciple of Qāḍīzāde".

[4] On these prayers and the Ottoman controversies concerning their lawful or prohibited nature, see Kātib Çelebi, *Mīzān*, trans. Lewis, *Balance*, pp. 97–100; S. Çavuşoğlu, *Movement*, pp. 248–252.

[5] On these invocations and the Ottoman controversies concerning them, see Kātib

ff. 77v–84v; *Kılıç Ali Paşa 1035*, ff. 69v–70r; *Reisülküttab 1182*, ff. 57v–64r; *Reşid Efendi 985*, ff. 87v–92r; *Şehid Ali Paşa 1189*, ff. 98r–104r. Yazmalar: Manisa İHK, *Akhisar Zeynelzade Koleksiyon*, 45 Ak Ze 5998/2, ff. 20v–29r (1310/1891).

14) *Risāla fī anna l-muṣāfaḥa ba'da l-ṣalawāt al-khamsa bid'a makrūha – Epistle explaining that shaking hands after the five prayers is a detestable innovation.*[1] MSS. *Harput 429*, ff. 72r–73r; *Reisülküttab 1182*, ff. 64v–65r. See also *Esad Efendi 3599*, ff. 218v–237v (same *incipit* but longer and other *explicit*). Yazmalar: Manisa İHK, *Akhisar Zeynelzade Koleksiyon*, 45 Ak Ze 1602/12, ff. 123r–v; 45 Ak Ze 6548/5, ff. 62r–63v (1311/1892).

15) *Risāla fī ḥurmat al-raqṣ wa l-dawarān – Epistle on the prohibition of dancing and whirling*. MS. *Harput 429*, ff. 65r–72r.[2] See also *Hafid Efendi 453*, ff. 79r–85r, which ends differently.

16) *Risāla fī l-radd 'alā maqābiriyya – Epistle refuting the visitors of tombs*. Or *Radd al-Qabriyya – Refutation of the visitors of tombs*.[3] MSS. *Fatih 5398*, ff. 71r–86v; *Hafid Efendi 453*, ff. 90r–117v; *Harput 429*, ff. 100r–118v; *Kılıç Ali Paşa 1035*, ff. 49v–68r. Yazmalar: Manisa, *İHK*, 45 Hk 2937/1, ff. 3v–20v.

17) *Risāla fī ḥukm al-dukhān – Epistle on the* [*Legal*] *status of tobacco* [*smoking*]. Or *Risāleh dukhāniyyeh – Epistle on tobacco*.[4] MSS. *Darülmesnevi 258*, ff. 70v–74v; *Harput 429*, ff. 194v–199v; *Kılıç Ali Paşa 1035*, ff. 31v–36v; *Reisülküttab 1182*, ff. 52v–57r. See also the extract copied in MS. *Giresun 114* (28 Hk 3587/7), p. 27: *Maṭlab fī*

Çelebi, *Mīzān*, trans. Lewis, *Balance*, pp. 47–49; S. Çavuşoğlu, *Movement*, pp. 238–244.

1 On shaking hands after the prayer and the Ottoman controversies concerning it, see Kātib Çelebi, *Mīzān*, trans. Lewis, *Balance*, pp. 101–102; S. Çavuşoğlu, *Movement*, pp. 231–236.

2 On the Ottoman controversies concerning Sufi dancing, notably Khalwatī, see Kātib Çelebi, *Mīzān*, trans. Lewis, *Balance*, pp. 42–46; S. Çavuşoğlu, *Movement*, pp. 194–207.

3 On the Ottoman controversies concerning the visiting of tombs, see Kātib Çelebi, *Mīzān*, trans. Lewis, *Balance*, pp. 92–96; S. Çavuşoğlu, *Movement*, pp. 302–307.

4 On the Ottoman controversies concerning tobacco, see Kātib Çelebi, *Mīzān*, trans. Lewis, *Balance*, pp. 50–59; S. Çavuşoğlu, *Movement*, pp. 215–224.

ḥaqq al-dukhān – Inquiry concerning tobacco. Yazmalar: Manisa İHK, *Akhisar Zeynelzade Koleksiyon*, 45 Ak Ze 1602/1, ff. I + 1v–6r; *İHK*, 45 Hk 2937/5, ff. 43r–47v.

Beginning of the Risāleh dukhāniyyeh[1]

18) *Risāla fī l-ṭā'ūn – Epistle on the plague*. MS. *Harput 429*, ff. 164v–184v.

19) *Risāla fī l-arāḍī – Epistle on the* [*Legal nature*] *of lands*. MSS. *Ali Emiri Arabi 4343*, ff. 40–46 (1114/1702); *Darülmesnevi 258*, ff. 130v–137r; *Haci Beşir Ağa 662*, ff. 194v–204v; *Harput 429*, ff. 185r–194r; *Kasidecizade 682*, ff. 45v–57v (1089/1678); *Kılıç Ali Paşa 1035*, ff. 71v–80r; *Ragip Paşa 461*, ff. 154v–157v (1066/1655). Yazmalar: Manisa, *İHK*, 45 Hk 2937/7, ff. 63v–71r.[2]

1 Left: MS. *Harput 429*, f. 194v. Right: MS. *Darülmesnevi 258*, f. 70v.

2 On other lists of al-Aqḥiṣārī's works, see Y. Michot, *Opium*, p. 55, n. 1; M. Eryarsoy & M. el-Humeyyis, *Risaleleri*, p. 11. The *Daqā'iq al-ḥaqā'iq – Subtle Truths* mentioned by M. E. Müderrisoğlu (*Akhisarlı*, p. 53) and M. Eryarsoy & M. el-Humeyyis (*Risaleleri*, p. 11) is obviously anterior to al-Aqḥiṣārī as it already appears in the MS. *Haci Mahmud Efendi 2248* copied in 924/1518.

There is nothing peculiar in the fact that an Ottoman religious scholar like al-Aqḥiṣārī was interested in writing on the Qur'ān and the *Ḥadīth*, monotheism and prophethood, worship, spiritual wayfaring and submission to religious authorities. As for the topics dealt with in several of his other writings, how could they leave the historian indifferent? The dual nature of innovations, Raghā'ib and Berāt prayers, the remembrance of God (*dhikr*), the invoking of divine blessings during the Friday sermon, shaking hands after the collective prayer, Sufi dancing and whirling, the visiting of tombs and tobacco are indeed some of the very hot issues having divided Qāḍīzādelis and their Sufi opponents. With the exception of *dhikr*, Kātib Çelebi notably devotes a chapter of his amazing *Balance of Truth* to every one of them.[1] Now, needless to say, on each of these issues, al-Aqḥiṣārī does not appear to have been among those whom Kātib Çelebi calls "the intelligent ones", i.e. those who kept out of "a profitless quarrel, born of fanaticism".[2] He rather seems to have been, on all these issues, among the "foolish people" persistently attached to one side, in this case, as easily predictable, that of the strict ulema and prohibitionists who shared in some measure the views of Qāḍīzāde, Birgivī, Ibn Qayyim and Ibn Taymiyya.

The present book is devoted to one of al-Aqḥiṣārī's epistles, namely his *Risāleh dukhāniyyeh – Epistle on tobacco*. The choice of this particular text has probably no other reason than the interest in the use of drugs in Islamic societies that has already led me to translate Ibn Taymiyya's fatwā on cannabis and to study opium addiction and coffee in Ottoman Turkey.[3] Besides tobacco, al-Aqḥiṣārī indeed also has something to say about these three substances in his *Dukhāniyyeh*. Before presenting this particular epistle, it will be worthwhile taking a little time to explore further the age and personality of its author.

1 R. Peters (*Dervishes*, p. 114, n. 38) draws attention to the identity of the table of contents of Kātib Çelebi's *Balance* with the list of Q ạ̄ḍīzāde's controversial opinions given by the Ottoman historian M. Na'īma (d. 1128/1716).

2 See Kātib Çelebi, *Mīzān*, trans. Lewis, *Balance*, p. 133.

3 See Y. Michot, *Haschich, Opium*.

THE COMPLEXITIES OF A RADICAL PIETISM

AL-AQḤIṢĀRĪ lived in a period marked by a financial crisis around 1008–9/1600, by the disintegration of the imperial Ottoman authority and the corruption of the elites, by a deep societal unrest and by grave tension between popular mosque preachers and medresse ulema, puritanical zealots and licentious or innovating shaykhs.[1] The hundred topics entered upon in his *Majālis* show that he is mainly concerned with personal piety, commercial righteousness, religious and social issues, rather than with affairs of court, political and military matters.

1 The remembrance of God (*dhikr Allāh*)
2 The eminence of *dhikr*
3 The eminence of faith
4 Love of the Prophet
5 Faith in his teachings
6 Tasting the savour of faith
7 Faith in the Prophet
8 Obeying and disobeying the Prophet
9 Following the Prophet
10 Believer (*mu'min*), *Muslim*, *mujāhid*...
11 The best *dhikr* and invocations
12 The intercession of the Prophet
13 Pure monotheism (*ikhlāṣ al-tawḥīd*)
14 The faith that will save
15 The natural state of Islam (*fiṭrat al-islām*)
16 The various kinds of unbelief
17 The prohibition of praying near tombs
18 The various kinds of innovations
19 *Raghā'ib* & other innovated prayers
20 The eminence of *ḥajj* & its innovations
21 The eminence of almsgiving & forsaking it
22 The eminence of fasting
23 The eminence of fasting in *Sha'bān*
24 *Laylat al-barā'a*: *sunna* and innovations
25 The sighting of the Ramaḍān new moon
26 Ramaḍān
27 Intention, fasting, breaking the fast
28 *Tarāwiḥ* prayers
29 Delaying the prayer and breaking the fast
30 Expiation for breaking the fast
31 Ramaḍān retreat & *Laylat al-Qadr*
32 *Ṣadaqat al-fiṭr*, the Feasts & innovations
33 Fasting in *Shawwāl*
34 The ten first days of *Dhū l-Ḥijja*
35 The sacrifice
36 *Muḥarram* and *'Āshūrā'* fasting
37 *'Āshūrā'*: traditions and innovations
38 Curing the sick
39 Evil & good omens, blameworthy & *sunnī*
40 Brotherhood in this world's affairs
41 Disasters, repentance and invocations
42 Repelling disasters with invocations
43 Praying in case of frights
44 Prayers for the solar and lunar eclipses
45 Praying for rain
46 Learning the prescriptions and Qur'ān
47 Recitation of the Qur'ān
48 The call to prayer
49 The eminence of Friday
50 Shaking hands
51 The obligation of prayer
52 The obligation of praying as prescribed
53 The five daily prayers and expiation
54 The eminence of collective prayer
55 Funeral prayer
56 Saying *Lā ilāha illā Llāh* and Paradise
57 The visitation of tombs
58 Remembering death and getting ready
59 The plague and prophylaxis
60 Patience in case of plague
61 The eminence of patience and disasters
62 On the *ḥadīth* "Collect five things..."
63 The calling of servants to account
64 Calling oneself to account before death
65 Inviting the *umma* to repent now
66 On "God accepts the repentance..."

[1] See M. C. Zilfi, *Politics*, especially pp. 30–31, 90–91.

67 The intelligent and the foolish
68 Piety (*taqwā*) and good character
69 Lawful earnings
70 The prohibition of monopolies
71 The fates of traders in the hereafter
72 Trading, truthfulness and trustfulness
73 The true nature of usury
74 Forward buying (*salam*) & other contracts
75 Begging
76 The rights of slaves
77 The prohibition of homosexuality
78 The prohibition of drinking wine
79 The prohibition of cheating (*fulūl*)
80 The appearing of troubles (*fitna*)
81 Judges, bribes & false testimonies
82 Who should be appointed preacher
83 The renewers of the religion, every century
84 Eminence of greeting another the first
85 Turning away from a Muslim brother
86 The prohibition of low opinion and spying
87 Frequenting perverts and eating with them
88 The best deed: loving and hating for God
89 The Prophet's commands and prohibitions
90 The preeminence of God's mercy
91 "Satan circulates in man like his blood"
92 Being tempted is not punished
93 Satan and the angel are close to man
94 Islam started as something foreign
95 The grace of good health
96 Not entering the mosque if smelling bad
97 What one should not be interested in
98 Recommendation concerning women
99 The *ḥadīth* "Ask for advice of women…"
100 Women's obligations

The pious, rigorist admonitions of the *Majālis* are thus not primarily intended for a prince or a ruler but, rather, for the *petit bourgeois* milieu of Ottoman bazaaris, ulema and civil servants. Sometimes however, the reader notices criticisms of the authorities, of their deficiencies or of their excesses. Like several of al-Aqḥiṣārī's epistles, some chapters of his *Majālis* also remind one of subjects dealt with by Kātib Çelebi in his *Mīzān*: the use of music for religious purposes (*Majlis* XLVII), tobacco (*Majlis* XCVI–XCVII), innovations (*Majlis* XVIII, etc.), pilgrimages to tombs (*Majlis* XVII, LVII), supererogatory prayers (*Majlis* XIX), shaking hands (*Majlis* L), enjoining right and forbidding wrong (*Majlis* LXXXIX), bribery (*Majlis* LXXXI).

According to the famous Delhi theologian Shāh 'Abd al-'Azīz (d. 1239/1824): "The *Book of the Councils of the Pious and the Paths of the Best*, on the science of exhortation (*wa'ẓ*) and admonition (*naṣīḥa*), presents many benefits about the secrets of the *Sharī'a* prescriptions and about jurisprudence (*fiqh*), on the subjects of the [spiritual] way and on the topics concerning the refutation of innovations and blameworthy habits."[1] Al-Aqḥiṣārī's *Majālis* also offers wonderfully vivid echoes of the societal reality in which he lived, as well as direct manifestations of his own concerns vis-à-vis the evolution of Ottoman Turkey at the beginning of the 11th/17th century and clear insights into the nature of

1 Quote in S. B. al-Shikārpūrī, *Khazīna*, p. 615–616.

his reformist agenda. It is therefore appropriate to let him explain himself, about a few issues also tackled by Kātib Çelebi, what was going wrong and which solutions he favoured.

After weighing the arguments for or against religious singing, Kātib Çelebi concludes that "the intelligent man will not be so stupid as to hope to decide a dispute of such long standing."[1] In the *Majālis*, al-Aqḥiṣārī's opinion on the subject is clearcut: singing is an even greater sin than listening to singing, and finding it beautiful amounts to becoming an infidel. Such is in fact the status of all those preachers, muezzins and Sufis who indulge in music during their sermons, invocations, praises, and graces, and of those who go to mosques or frequent them in order to listen to them. Particularly interesting for the linguist, the musicologist and the historian of Ottoman religious practices, are the examples of word alterations of which our author then accuses the clerics and mystics of his time:

"Listening to singing (*taghannī*) is a major sin (*kabīra*) and someone singing for people brings them to commit this major sin together. As listening to singing is a major sin, that singing is a major sin is thus even more true. Someone singing thus also commits this major sin and the beauty which he puts in it amounts to making lawful that which is categorically forbidden; now this is unbelief (*kufr*). From this it is manifest that when one attends the Friday and collective prayers in our time, one hardly escapes committing a major sin. The sermons and the recitations of many of the preachers (*khaṭīb*) and the Qur'ān reciters are indeed rarely free from singing. On the contrary, in their sermons and their recitations, they adopt the ways that they follow with poems and ghazals, to the point that one almost does not understand what they say and what they recite, because of the melodic effects and the scansions. Such is also the situation with the muezzins in their blessings on the Prophet, their calls for God's satisfaction with others, their "*Amīn*s", and their "*Allāhu akbar*s" at the various intervals in the prayer. Those present who listen commit this major sin. Some of them or, rather, most of them, sometimes or, rather, most of the time, find them beautiful as

[1] Kātib Çelebi, *Mīzān*, trans. Lewis, *Balance*, p. 41.

the caprice of their soul predominates in them and they do not care about religious matters; from which it necessarily follows that they become unbelievers, according to what is related from Ẓahīr al-Dīn al-Marghīnānī.[1] Similarly for those who attend the *tarāwīḥ* prayers during the nights of Ramaḍān in order to listen to the songs of praises (*tasbīḥ*) of the muezzins, in the great and the small mosques. The names of God appearing in these [praises], like "O Compassionate!" (*yā ḥannān*), "O Kind!" (*yā mannān*), "O Liberal and Beneficent!" (*yā dhā l-jūd wa l-iḥsān*), and [phrases] like "Praised be the One Who possesses the Sovereignty and the Royalty! Praised be the One Who possesses the Power and the Empire!" (*subḥāna dhī l-mulk wa l-malakūt, subḥāna dhī l-'izza wa l-jabarūt*), and other of the most beautiful names and superior attributes, by multiplying the melodic and musical effects, they change them and they distort them to a degree where it is no longer possible to distinguish them and to identify them. They for instance say *sūbḥānā l-mālikī l-ḥānnān! sūbḥānā l-mālikī l-mānnān!* ("Prai-ai-ai-sed be-e-e th-th-the Com-m-mpassionate Ki-i-ing! Prai-ai-ai-sed be-e-e th-th-the Kind Ki-i-ing!"), by singularly lengthening the *u* following the *s*, the *a* following the *n* and the *m*, and the *i* following the *l* and the *k*, etc. Similar are the musical effects of the Sufis. They for instance say after the meals, as grace, *al-ḥamdū lī-Llāh! al-shukrū lī-Llāh!* ("Glory-y-y to-o-o God! Thanks-s-s to-o-o God!"), with long vowels after the *d*, the *r* and the *l*, etc. The Muslim ought to be wary of attending these things and hearing them, and shall look for a mosque that is free of them. Such things indeed have the appearence of worship but are in reality disobeying and a major sin. One perhaps even finds them beautiful and his religion is wiped out: he is not aware of it and the situation then is that ignorance will not be an excuse."[2]

No wonder that ulema sing in the mosques as, for al-Aqḥiṣārī, they are grievously sick. They themselves suffer from the diseases from which they are supposed to cure people. Moreover, instead of being

1 Ẓahīr al-Dīn al-Ḥasan b. 'Alī Abū l-Maḥāsin al-Marghīnānī (6th/12th c.), Ḥanafite jurist, teacher of Fakhr al-Dīn Qāḍīkhān (d. 592/1196) and Burhān al-Dīn al-Marghīnānī; see W. Heffening, *EI2*, art. al-Marghīnānī.

2 Al-Aqḥiṣārī, *Majālis,* XLVII, MS. *Michot 0402*, f. 128r–v.

moral guides reminding the commonalty of the Day of Judgement and Hell, they corrupt them even more by charming them and deluding them with idle hopes in the divine mercy. And what beats all, these worthless ulema often solicit a reward for their evil services! Al-Aqḥiṣārī's opposition to such clerical mercantilism once again brings him closer to Birgivī as the latter, according to Kātib Çelebi, declared in his *al-Sayf al-Ṣārim – The Sharp Sword*, "that it was unlawful to accept payment in return for reciting the Qur'ān, or for teaching, or indeed for any act of worship."[1]

"One almost does not understand what they say and what they recite, because of the melodic effects and the scansions. Such is also the situation with the muezzins in their blessings on the Prophet..."[2]

"The physicians, these are the ulema and, in this time, they have become sick, seriously sick, to the point of being unable to treat themselves, not to speak of treating others. This is the reason why the discase is general, the therapy has been interrupted, and the creatures are perishing. Or, rather, the physicians keep themselves busy with various

1 Kātib Çelcbi, *Mīzān*, trans. Lewis, *Balance*, p. 129.

2 Turkish miniatures (2nd half of the 11th/17th c.); from F. Taeschner, *Volksleben*, pls. 15, 45.

ways of misguiding [people]. Would to God, if only, as they do not improve matters, they were not corrupting them! If only they were keeping silent and were not talking! When they speak, in their religious exhortations, they indeed do not aim at anything else than to win the hearts of the commonalty. Now, they do not obtain access to them but by making mention of the hope [in God] and the [divine] mercy, as that is more pleasing to the ears and lighter on [human] nature. The creatures thus leave their councils of religious exhortation (*majlis wa'ẓ*) with, as sole profit, an overplus of insolence in committing actions of disobedience. Now, as long the physician is like that, the sick are led to perish because of the remedy, as it is administered in the wrong manner."[1] "One ought to know that when the ulema, in the councils which they devote to knowledge, solicit something from the people, doing so is not lawful for them, as this is earning something by means of a scholarly activity and an action of obedience [to God], no matter whether they solicit [it] for themselves or for others. Among the blameworthy solicitations is the fact of offering a little in order to take a lot, as is done when one is invited to weddings or circumcisions, as well as the fact of taking care of [someone else's] sheep with the intention of getting to keep its young, as it is said that it is about this that His words, Exalted is He, were sent down: "And show not favour, seeking wordly gain!"[2]

For Kātib Çelebi, "it is among the duties of the Sultan of the Muslims to subdue and discipline ranting fanatics [...], whoever they may be."[3] Alluding to situations where self-appointed, arrogant, ambitious, sanctimonious activists start taking preachers to task, al-Aqḥiṣārī speaks of the obligation that the authorities—in his case, the "imām", not "the sultan of the Muslims"—have to appoint knowledgeable clerics in villages and urban *maḥalla*s, after an examination, as would be the case with physicians, and in order to prevent people from innovating and going astray "as is happening in this time". For al-Aqḥiṣārī, that the religious guidance offered by the Ottoman ulema to their society at the

1 Al-Aqḥiṣārī, *Majālis,* LXXXII, MS. *Michot 0402*, f. 226v.

2 Qur'ān, *al-Mudaththir* - 74:6; al-Aqḥiṣārī, *Majālis,* LXXV, MS. *Michot 0402*, f. 207r.

3 Kātib Çelebi, *Mīzān*, trans. Lewis, *Balance*, p. 134.

beginning of the 11th/17th century is of such poor quality is thus not entirely their fault. This being so, rather than condoning seditious developments, he calls for a reform led by the authorities and reminds the latter of their duty towards their subjects:

"The third [type of individual] is the one feeling self important (*mukhtāl*). He is neither an emir, nor given orders (*ma'mūr*) in any way. He is rather an uncommissioned agent (*fuḍūlī*) and does that because of arrogance towards people and craving for leadership (*ri'āsa*). He gives them prescriptions and acts ostentatiously in front of them, in his sayings and actions, and, without the imām's authorization, prevents preachers (*wā'iẓ*) from exhorting [people]. This is so only because it is incumbent upon the imām to take care of the interests of [his] subjects and to appoint, in every village and in every city quarter (*maḥalla*), a devout scholar who will teach people their religion. He shall therefore examine the scholars: someone in whom he sees knowledge, religiousness and orthodoxy (*ḥusn 'aqīda*), he shall authorize him to exhort people; someone in whom he does not see these attributes, he shall not authorize him to exhort, so as not to make people fall into innovation and erring, as is happening in this time. And that [is necessary] because the creatures (*khalq*) are not born with knowledge: they are only born with ignorance. Now, ignorance is one of the diseases of the hearts. They therefore inevitably need a skilful physician to treat them and make their disease end by teaching them the regulations (*aḥkām*) of the religion, in its fundamentals and its derivative parts. Someone not skilful will indeed not make their disease end; he will rather increase it and thus make them perish. In [al-Ghazālī's] *Revivification* (*Iḥyā'*), it is mentioned that this world is the abode of the sick."[1]

To what extent al-Aqḥiṣārī really considers the Ottoman authorities capable of bringing order and value into the corps of ulema and preachers is open to question as, in another passage of the *Majālis*, he accuses these authorities of not following the Islamic Law and even calls them unbelievers. For all those who see the *Sharī'a* as a totalitarian system of law, it will be a surprise to read al-Aqḥiṣārī's call for its

1 Al-Aqḥiṣārī, *Majālis,* LXXXII, MS. *Michot 0402*, f. 226r.

implementation as a way to curb despotism and injustice. A barrier against tyranny, that is indeed how our author sees the "Muḥammadan Way/Law (*shar'*)", and the examples that he gives clearly prove his point. If, as he explicitly leads us to think, what al-Aqḥiṣārī has in mind is what was going on in Turkey in his time, the picture that he offers of Ottoman governmental and judiciary institutions around the beginning of the 11th/17th century is rather negative. Should one see in it an echo of the famously tough policies of Murād IV (1032/1623–1049/1640)? In the opinion of Kātib Çelebi, the puritanical injunctions of Birgivī "achieved nothing, as they were opposed to custom (*'urf*) and usage (*'ādat*)."[1] It is this same custom (*'urf*) which al-Aqḥiṣārī nevertheless considers the main cause of the injustice of the "governments" (*ḥukūmāt*) and of the "policies" (*siyāsāt*) which he criticizes, when the authorities take it as their exclusive rule of action or mix Islamic law with it. The sentence which our author then utters is peremptory: the preference which governants give to such alternatives to the *Shar'* excommunicates them. In saying that, he could be presented as being as radical as Ibn Taymiyya and Ibn Kathīr in their anathematizing the Mongol Īlkhāns for following the *Yasa* of Genghis Khān in preference to the *Sharī'a*, or as the modern Islamists fomenting rebellion against their goverments when the latter substitute foreign, man-made, legislations for the divine one.[2] Just like Ibn Taymiyya, Ibn Kathīr or these Islamists, al-Aqḥiṣārī most probably has in mind Qur'ānic verses like *al-Mā'ida* - 5:44: "Those who do not judge by what God has sent down—it is they who are the faithless." That being so, what deserves most particular attention is the fact that al-Aqḥiṣārī does not then urge any kind of armed opposition against unjust authorities but only commands passive, peaceable disobedience, to the point, if necessary, of accepting martyrdom at the hands of these authorities; which in fact also reminds us of Ibn Taymiyya, when the latter, like various other great classical ulema, was writing: "If a [religious scholar] is beaten, detained, and subjected to diverse sorts of hurt in order to [force him to]

1 Kātib Çelebi, *Mīzān*, p. 229; trans. Lewis, *Balance*, p. 131.

2 See Y. Michot, *Muslims*, pp. 49–50, 104–106.

abandon what he knows of the Law (*shar'*) of God and His Messenger, which he is under obligation to follow [...] it is incumbent upon him to be patient. If, in respect of God, he is subjected to some hurt, that is God's way of acting (*sunna*) with the Prophets and their followers. God indeed said: "Do men imagine that they will be left (at ease) because they say "We believe", and will not be tested with affliction?"[1]

"Sometimes, their king becomes angry with one of them and he commands [*his people*] *to kill him without any reason..."*[2]

"As injustice and corruption overcome them, it is also likely that the [authorities] do not comply with the Way/Law (*shar'*) in their governments (*ḥukūmāt*). Rather, they depart from it in favour of [various] species of injustice and policies (*siyāsāt*). They spill blood and seize properties without right and believe that they are right in committing these sins. And they do not know that, by believing that, they depart from Islam. Sometimes, they crucify the thief and kill him, believing that it is permitted to crucify him and to kill him. By believing that, they

1 Qur'ān, *al-'Ankabūt* - 29:2; see Ibn Taymiyya, *MF*, vol. xxxv, p. 374.

2 *The Death of Mustapha*. Engraving in J. A. Guer, *Mœurs*, vol. ii, p. 470.

become unbelievers because the [Legal] punishment (*ḥadd*), for the thief, is not to crucify him and to kill him. Rather, his punishment is to cut off his hand, because of His words, Exalted is He: "As for the thief, both male and female, cut off their hands."[1] Sometimes, their king becomes angry with one of them and he commands [his people] to kill him without any [Legal] reason obliging his killing. So they kill him, believing that his command is right, and a duty for them (*wājib 'alay-him*). By believing that, they become unbelievers, as "[There is] no obedience to a creature while disobeying the Creator", according to what is reported in the *ḥadīth*.[2]

"A simple command of the sultan, without intimidation or threat, is coercion (*ikrāh*). So, since it is coercion, is it an allowance (*rakhkhaṣa*) made for [his people] to kill [this person]?" If this is said, the answer will be that to kill a Muslim without right is not made lawful by any [situation of] constraint (*ḍarūra*), as mentioned about coercion in the *Commentary* on *The Guidance* (*al-Hidāya*):[3] someone coerced, under threat of being killed, to kill somebody else without right, is not allowed to give himself precedence [in the matter]. He will rather be patient to the point of [letting himself] be killed. To kill the [other] would indeed be a sin because to kill a Muslim without right is among the things that are not made permissible by any [situation of] constraint—and similarly for coercion. In the fundamentals [of jurisprudence] (*uṣūl*), it is mentioned that a reason (*dalīl*) for making allowance (*rukhṣa*) is the fear of perishing. Now, the killer and his victim to be are equal in this and, as they both are equal [therein], it is not lawful, for the agent,[4] to kill someone else in order to save himself. God, Exalted is He, indeed made it a very serious offence to kill a Muslim when He said: "Who kills a believer of set purpose, his reward is hell forever."[5] This being so, one

1 Qur'ān, *al-Mā'ida* - 5:38.

2 See al-Bukhārī, *Ṣaḥīḥ*, *Āḥād*, *bāb* 1 (Bulaq, vol. ix, p. 88); Muslim, *Ṣaḥīḥ*, *Imāra*, 39 (Constantinople, vol. vi, p. 15); Ibn Ḥanbal, *Musnad*, vol. i, p. 94.

3 *Al-Hidāya fī l-furū'*, by the Ḥanafite jurist Burhān al-Dīn 'Alī b. Abī Bakr al-Marghīnānī (d. 593/1197).

4 *al-fā'il*. Perhaps a mistake for *al-qātil*, "the killer", which is graphically similar.

5 Qur'ān, *al-Nisā'* - 4:93.

must know that many of the authorities (*walī*) of our time and of the qāḍīs of our age have gone out of (*hajara*) the Muḥammadan Way/Law (*shar'*) and invented (*aḥdatha*) an unsatisfactory path, which they called "custom" (*'urf*). Acting on its basis has so spread among them that the Way/Law (*shar'*) is almost refused. Indeed, they do not decide a case by simply [following] the Way/Law (*bi-maḥḍ al-shar'*), without mixing custom [with it], but they decide many cases by simply [following] custom (*bi-maḥḍ al-'urf*), without mixing the Way/Law [with it]! And they believe that, by simply [following] the Way/Law, order (*niẓām*) will not be achieved and the situation of humans will not be made right. They say so openly and they do not consider it reprehensible!"[1]

The excerpts of the *Majālis* translated above relate to the religious, judiciary, and governmental establishments. Many other passages would confirm the breadth of al-Aqḥiṣārī's reformism but three will suffice here. They relate to homosexuality, the education of slaves, and crafts.

"In this time, [homosexuality] has spread in this Muḥammadan community and expanded among its Arabs and its non-Arabs, its learned ones and its ignorant ones, its elite and its commonalty. It has reached such a point that they are proud of it and blame someone who has no beardless friend (*amrad*), speak evil of him, and say that he is not a human (*adamī*) and has no taste (*madhāq*). They are proud of having a beardless friend standing before them and they dress him with the best clothes, made of prohibited [stuff], so that they might be seen in their best disposition."[2]

"Just as it is obligatory on the Muslim to spend on his slaves, males and females, an amount sufficing them, it is obligatory on him to teach them the duties that God Most High has imposed on them and what He has prohibited to them. Now, this is an affair that most of the ulema, in this time, have themselves neglected, not to speak of the commonalty! In this time, fundamentally no attention is given to teaching the slaves, males and females. Rather, attention is only given to them in relation to the exclusive attainment of worldly aims, as if they were, in the eyes of

1 Al-Aqḥiṣārī, *Majālis,* LXXX, MS. *Michot 0402*, f. 221r–v.

2 Al-Aqḥiṣārī, *Majālis,* LXXVII, MS. *Michot 0402*, f. 212v.

their owners, animals, beasts not submitted to any religious obligations (*lā taklīf ʻalay-him*). Many of those who, in this time, claim to be Muslims, have a number of slaves, males and females. They however do not command them anything obligatory nor prohibit to them anything forbidden. Moreover, the male slave and the slave girl might be in the possession of someone for a number of years, without praying the compulsory prayers and busy committing many among the prohibited things and the reprehensible ones: he sees them both, does not mind and thinks that their sin is upon them both, not upon him. This poor man does not know that what emanates from them will be held against him, that he is responsible for it and that he will be punished for it."[1]

"Amongst the crafts, there are some that are important and some that can be dispensed with as they amount to seeking to brag (*tanaffuj*) and preen during the life in this world. It is thus incumbent upon one to be occupied with an important craft so as, by practising it, to make up for the shortcomings of the Muslims in important matters concerning the religion. One shall not be occupied with the crafts of painting, goldsmithing, and all those by means of which life in this world is ornamented. It is mentioned, in *The Choice* (*al-Ikhtiyār*),[2] that the most eminent means of earning a living is commerce, then agriculture, then craftmanship."[3]

A comprehensive understanding of the complexities of al-Aqḥiṣārī's spiritual radicalism and a precise positioning of his views in the moving landscape of Islamic pietist reformism, from the classical period to modern times, would obviously require much further research and are not the objective pursued here. As for getting some idea of the reasons why al-Aqḥiṣārī also authored a *Risāleh dukhāniyyeh – Epistle on tobacco*, the few pages of the *Majālis* translated above provide a very useful clue: for such a rigorist reformer, the introduction of tobacco into an Ottoman empire already perceived by him as going astray must have meant a societal cataclysm of satanic proportions!

1 Al-Aqḥiṣārī, *Majālis*, LXXVI, MS. *Michot 0402*, f. 209v.

2 *Al-Ikhtiyār li-taʻālīl al-mukhtār*, by the Ḥanafite jurist ʻAbd Allāh b. Maḥmūd b. Mawdūd al-Mawṣilī (d. 683/1284).

3 Al-Aqḥiṣārī, *Majālis*, LXIX, MS. *Michot 0402*, f. 186v.

HOW TO TURN DOWN AN ENGLISH PRESENT

IN French and Italian, "fumer comme un Turc", "fumare come un Turco", i.e. "to smoke like a Turk", are time-honoured expressions. Things might change as, since January 3, 2008, Law No. 5727 bans smoking in indoor public places in Turkey. A new phase has thus begun in the intense debates about the harmfulness or benefits of tobacco that have deeply divided the Turkish society, its ruling authorities and its religious scholars, during the last four centuries. Unlike their passion for opium, the Ottomans' love-hate relationship with tobacco has been the object of serious academic research.[1] One can, accordingly, dispense with recalling here the evolution of this relationship, from the first arrival of tobacco in Turkey at the end of the tenth/sixteenth century to the short-lived despotic prohibitions of Murad IV (r. 1032/1623–1049/1640) and a final acceptance of smoking. As for the importance of the societal impact of the new intoxication in the Ottoman empire, it could not be underlined enough, as pertinently noted by J. Grehan.[2] Both in relation to an hedonistic use of the organism and to more relaxed patterns of social interaction, tobacco smoking indeed confirmed and deepened the transformations initiated among the Ottomans, one century earlier, by the spread of coffee and the *kahvekhānes*. "The pivotal role of tobacco was to broaden and further entrench this public culture of fun."[3]

1 See notably E. Bakla, *Tophane* (with splendid illustrations); A. Saraçgıl, *Generi*, pp. 170–192; F. Klein-Franke, *Smoking*; L. Berger, *Herz*; B. Lewis, *Istanbul*, pp. 132–136; the synthesis of J. Grehan, *Smoking*.

2 See J. Grehan, *Smoking*, p. 1353. For Grehan, tobacco thus helped the Ottoman Middle East to "acquire some of the most salient characteristics of an "early modern" culture". Insofar as the terminology is appropriate, one could argue further that this "early modernization" had already started not only during the sixteenth century with the Arabian nectar but even earlier, under the Mamlūks, with cannabis; see Y. Michot, *Haschich*, pp. 54–59.

3 J. Grehan, *Smoking*, p. 1375. "One has to imagine that tobacco smoking [...] was accompanied by the constant noise of sneezing, suckling and spitting. The conservative among the Muslims certainly felt disgusted" (F. Klein-Franke, *Smoking*, p. 158).

"It is an amusement, and moreover a pleasure of aesthetic taste..."[1]

A. 'U. Āl Salmān gives the titles of some ninety works written by past Muslim scholars for or against tobacco, including al-Aqḥiṣārī's *Dukhāniyyeh.*[2] Although the arguments feeding the polemic in these works have been the object of various studies,[3] few of the texts themselves have been edited,[4] and the translations available in European languages are all but inexistent.[5] Hence the decision to offer here both an *editio princeps* and a complete English version of al-Aqḥiṣārī's

[1] I. Peçevi, quoted in B. Lewis, *Istanbul*, p. 134. Smokers, Turkey, 11th/17th c. Left: miniature from MS. *A.365*, *Costumi orientali*, Bologna, Biblioteca Comunale dell'Archiginnasio. Right: miniature from F. Taeschner, *Volksleben*, pl. 36.

[2] A. 'U. Āl Salmān, *Ta'līqāt*, pp. 93–108; see no. 42.

[3] See J. Grehan, *Smoking*, pp. 1359–1362, 1369–1373; M. b. J. al-Kattānī, *I'lān*; F. Klein-Franke, *Smoking*; L. Berger, *Herz*; R. Matthee, *Pursuit*, pp. 135–137 (the Shī'ī Persian tobacco controversies).

[4] For example 'Abd al-Nāfi', *Takhlīṣ*; Karīm al-Dīn Ḥusayn al-Azharī, *Ḥukm*; Ibrāhīm al-Laqānī, *Naṣīḥa*; Mar'ī b. Yūsuf al-Karmī, *Taḥqīq*; Kātib Çelebī, *Mīzān*; 'Abd al-Ghanī al-Nābulusī, *Ibāḥa*.

[5] In *Solaz*, pp. 141–169, I. Lozano translates excerpts of three texts by Muslim authors of the 17th–18th centuries. In *Herz*, L. Berger translates and studies several passages of I. al-Laqānī, *Naṣīḥa*, and 'A. Gh. al-Nābulusī, *Ibāḥa*. Kātib Çelebī's *Mīzān* is translated by G. L. Lewis, *Balance*.

epistle. In the remaining part of this Introduction, after an outline of the *Dukhāniyyeh*'s content, our author's treatment of the question of tobacco-smoking will be approached from two angles. First, an investigation into the relationship between this epistle and two *Councils* of the *Majālis* on the same topic. Second, a brief situation of the *Dukhāniyyeh* vis-à-vis three writings on tobacco also dating from the early part of the 11th/17th century.

Al-Aqḥiṣārī's *Dukhāniyyeh* is a fatwā-like text in which the author both formulates the question and provides an answer; in this case: is it lawful to use tobacco or is it obligatory to keep away from it? (lines 1–7 of the edition and translation). As for coffee, opium and cannabis before it, there is no scriptural text, Qur'ānic or Prophetic, that makes tobacco as clearly *ḥarām* as wine or gambling. Hence the necessity for prohibitionist ulema to invent an arsenal of arguments whose strength and converging nature might come to constitute a canonic interdiction.[1] The *Dukhāniyyeh* offers such an argumentation (l. 7–153) plus, and this makes it particularly interesting, a sort of meta-jurisprudential deliberation developed in two stages. First (l. 154–211), in an approach mixing socio-cultural history and comparative *fiqh*, al-Aqḥiṣārī relates the tobacco "calamity" (*fitna*) to the ones that, in earlier times, developed about *banj*, i.e. cannabis (l. 157–183), coffee (l. 184–198) and opium (l. 199–211). Second, as if the matter was one of principles of jurisprudence (*uṣūl al-fiqh*), the *Dukhāniyyeh* ends with a justification of its author's methodology from two points of view (l. 212–245): independent legal thinking (*ijtihād*) is still religiously admissible in the 11th/17th century,[2] and the prohibition of tobacco is in fact less a matter of analogic comparison (*qiyās*) with other prohibited substances than of deduction (*takhrīj*) from a universal rule.

Al-Aqḥiṣārī's arguments against tobacco are drawn from the Qur'ān, medicine, *ḥadīth* and distrust towards the West.

1 See F. Klein-Franke, *Smoking*, pp. 155–156.

2 On the relationship between "fundamentalism" and the claim that the gate of *ijtihād* is still open, through the basic notion of equality of believers, see the remarks of R. Peters, *Dervishes*, pp. 100–101.

In the Qur'ān, he finds a condemnation of futility, amusement and caprice. Useless for both this world and the next, tobacco must necessarily belong to one of these three types of things and is therefore also prohibited (l. 7–18). Later on (l. 94), whilst denouncing buying tobacco, an expensive commodity, as a "waste of one's wealth", he will briefly come back to the Qur'ān, in this case the scriptural prohibition of prodigality (*isrāf*). Finally (l. 119–134), it is verses linking fire, smoke and divine punishments which he will appeal to in order to justify his prohibitionist stand.

Health considerations play a remarkable part in al-Aqḥiṣārī's argumentation (l. 19–57). He uses medicine as a servant of jurisprudence, in order to demonstrate tobacco's harmfulness to the body, hence its prohibited nature, and quotes Avicenna and Galen as well as the Ḥanafite jurist al-Sunnāmī. He does not allow himself to be impressed by three objections of medical character and refutes them with a lot of common sense and foresight, referring to the opinions and practice of physicians as well as to the model of appropriate prudence vis-à-vis potential physiological and social harms embodied in the Qur'ānic prohibition of wine and gambling. He is fully aware that tobacco is among the things whose Legal "status is unclear" and can become the object of controversies among the ulema. Two principles, or rules, should therefore be followed (l. 58–93). One, the prohibition of something is proportional to its harmfulness. Now, in the particular case of tobacco, this harmfulness is "established by the reports of the most skilled of the physicians". Two, when the status of a thing is unclear, the Prophet recommended caution and abstaining from it, in order to preserve one's religion and honour. The less negative judgement that could be issued about tobacco would therefore still make it religiously *makrūh*, "detested". A last (pseudo-)medical objection could be that tobacco is a panacea. For our author, this notion, *per se*, does not make sense, and people seeing a universal remedy in tobacco are led astray by the Devil.

Al-Aqḥiṣārī uses two main types of Prophetic traditions against smoking. A first type has to do with bad smells (l. 95–118). Muḥammad's love of perfumes is well known. It is therefore not surprising that he forbade believers whose breath smelled of onions, garlic or leeks from coming near to his mosque or, even, ordered their expulsion.[1] For our author, this prohibition must in fact be extended to every abominable stink and every mosque, everywhere, out of respect for non-smokers.[2] It is even more relevant in the case of tobacco as, unlike the mentioned vegetables, it is not food. As for the second type of Prophetic traditions (l. 135–145), they either refer to the Prophet's dislike for hot food ("God Most High did not feed us fire!") or speak of divine punishments like some of the Qur'ānic verses already alluded to, but this time in a more eschatological perspective, by assimilating smokers to the People of Fire, at the end of time or in hell. Now, a believer should have nothing in common with such people.

"I could stand longer to persuade the world of some wonders that I have seen effected with one draught of excellent Tabacco*..."*[3]

Finally (l. 146–153), the fact that, according to al-Aqḥiṣārī, tobacco was introduced into the Muslim world by ill-intentioned infidels – more

[1] See F. Klein-Franke, *Smoking*, pp. 161–162; 'Abd al-Nāfi', *Takhlīṣ*, pp. 174, 176; al-Azharī, *Ḥukm*, p. 188.

[2] Unlike al-Azharī (*Ḥukm*, pp. 185–186), al-Aqḥiṣārī does not explicitly extend the interdiction to every mosque but assumes such extension.

[3] A. Chute, *Tabacco*, p. 16 (London, 1595). Left: Tobacco plant, drawing from *ibid.*, p. 35. Right: European smoker, drawing from *ibid.*, p. 15.

precisely, the English –, is a reason good enough to keep totally away from it. The problem is however that people, in his time, are "rigid and reluctant to comply" with the prescriptions of the religion and the guidance of the ulema.

Among the three other toxic substances which al-Aqḥiṣārī speaks about in his *Dukhāniyyeh*, it is *banj* which draws his attention first and longest. Like tobacco, this plant was unknown to the Prophet and the first Muslim generations. As soon as the recreational use of it reached alarming proportions, its corruptive power was recognised by Shāfi'ite scholars and it was duly prohibited by them. Our Ḥanafite scholar gives the impression of regretting that the authorities of his own school were slower to condemn the drug and seems relieved that they eventually did so. He admits that this condemnation is less severe than the Qur'ānic interdiction of wine but uses it anyway as a precedent for the prohibition of smoking.

Coffee does not deserve more mercy in al-Aqḥiṣārī's opinion. Most probably thinking of the free and often licentious atmosphere of the *kahvekhānes* of his time, he underlines the immorality of the setting in which coffee was then generally drunk. Another good reason to keep totally away from it is, for him, its harmful effect on the body. Many ulema have therefore prohibited it, including the famous 16th century Sheykhülislām Ebüssuūd from whom he borrows a fatwā denouncing the "debauchery" spreading with the "calamitous" vogue of this new beverage.

Al-Aqḥiṣārī's stand about opium and similar "corruptive substances" is quite ambiguous and surprisingly less severe than about coffee, cannabis and tobacco. On the one hand, he declares them prohibited and considers consuming them a sin. On the other hand, he allows the opium addict to continue to indulge a little if not doing so would put his life in danger. Moreover, and although he would prefer people in no need of it to keep away from it, he does not object to them taking a little, with or without good cause, as long as it does not muddle their reason and senses.

Our scholar's line about coffee and opium is thus the exact opposite of that of the author of the Ottoman text edited and studied in my

L'opium et le café: an unreserved condemnation of the drug and praise of the Arabian nectar.[1] Notwithstanding al-Aqḥiṣārī's ambiguity about the narcotic, his prohibition of coffee as well as of cannabis and tobacco makes him once more very close to the Qāḍīzādelis.[2]

"In the markets and bazaars too their pipes never left their hands..."[3]

RECYCLING ONE'S OWN WRITINGS

COUNCIL XCVI of the *Majālis* elaborates on the *ḥadīth* "Whoever eats of this stinking plant shall not at all come near to our mosque..."; *Council XCVII*, on the Prophetic tradition inviting Muslims to give up what should not concern them. Although these two councils are placed one after the other and refer to *ḥadīths* addressing two different

[1] On this text and its author, see the Appendix, p. 83.

[2] On the Qāḍīzādeli condemnation of coffee and tobacco, see S. Çavuşoğlu, *Movement*, pp. 63–64.

[3] I. Peçevi, quoted in B. Lewis, *Istanbul*, p. 134. Istanbul's Egyptian Bazaar, *The Illustrated London News*, 15 October 1853, p. 321.

issues, al-Aqḥiṣārī gives them an almost identical content. Besides short introductions and conclusions, in both cases he indeed appears to do little more than quote a long excerpt of the *Dukhāniyyeh*. He may omit some paragraphs, add a few sentences and make a number of minor changes; essentially, it is however the first 151 lines of his epistle that are easily recognized twice in the *Majālis*. There are several textual differences between the two abridged versions of the *Dukhāniyyeh* constituting *Councils XCVI* and *XCVII* but they are not really significant. Of far greater import would have been a thorough rewriting, in the *Majālis*, of the text that it twice borrows from the epistle, with a view, possibly, to a different readership or audience. One is bound to note however that nothing of the kind happened. The most interesting feature distinguishing the borrowed text of the two *Councils* and the *Dukhāniyyeh* is consequently that it ends twice at line 151. In other words, the remarks on the calamities of *banj*, coffee and opium, the laxism of Ḥanafites and the rigour of Shāfi'ites, independent legal thinking (*ijtihād*), analogy (*qiyās*) and deduction (*takhrīj*) with which al-Aqḥiṣārī ends his epistle are particular to the latter and absent from the *Majālis*. Is that because they were of too socio-historical, or too technical, a nature?

Tables of correspondences between the *Majālis* and the *Dukhāniyyeh*

Majlis XCVI[1]	***Dukhāniyyeh***
F. 261v, l. 22 – f. 262r, l. 8, ...*wa qad ruwiya*: Introduction	-------

Council XCVI, making clear the interdiction, for whoever has eaten something in which there is an abominable smell, to enter a mosque. – The Messenger of God – may God Most High bless him and grant him peace – said: "Whoever eats of this stinking plant shall not at all come near to our mosque. Indeed, the angels are offended by that which humans are offended by." This authentic *ḥadīth* of *al-Maṣābīḥ* is reported by Abū Hurayra. The demonstrative adjective ["this"] occurring in it refers to the [whole] genus of that which has an abominable smell, and the meaning is: "Whoever eats one of the things that have an abominable smell

[1] The foliation and lineation indicated are those of the MS. *Michot 0402* (**M**). For a description of this manuscript, see Y. Michot, *Opium*, pp. 56–61.

shall not at all come near to our mosque." What is apparent, from the [use of] the personal adjective ["our"], is that what is meant by "[our] mosque" is the mosque of the Prophet – may God bless him and grant him peace! The majority [of scholars] however said that it has a general [meaning, including] every mosque, since [the Prophet], blessing and peace be upon him, said in another *ḥadīth*: "…shall not at all come near to the mosques". They even included therein every meeting in pursuit of goodness (*majma‘ al-khayr*), like a council for knowledge (*majlis ‘ilm*), places where the Feast prayer is performed, funeral services, etc., as the reason [for the mentioned interdiction], i.e. offending the angels and the humans, is also to be found there. Furthermore, this is not an interdiction to enter a mosque and to attend collective prayers, because collective prayers are a confirmed tradition (*sunna mu'akkada*) similar to an obligation. It is therefore not appropriate to abstain from them by using something making it forbidden to attend them. This is rather an interdiction to consume anything making it forbidden to enter a mosque and to attend collective prayers. It is reported…

EXHALING THROUGH THE NOSE. [1]

TURK SMOKING.

F. 262r, l. 8, *anna-hu ‘alay-hi…* –> l. 12, *…yalzamu*

L. 101, *anna-hu ‘alay-hi…* –> l. 105, *…yalzamu*

…that when [the Prophet], blessing and peace be upon him, was finding… –> …it is consequently obligatory…

F. 262r, l. 12, *an yumna‘a…* –> l. 19, *…aṣlan*: composite passage

----

…to forbid from coming near to a mosque whoever consumes [this] tobacco (*dukhān*) which has appeared in this time, originating from the infidels, the enemies of the people of faith, and by which the whole of mankind is afflicted, be it the elite or the commonalty, as the abomination of its smell is more intense than the abomination of the smell of onions and garlic. Or, even, it is obligatory to expel

[1] Drawings in E. R. Billings, *Tobacco*, pp. 97, 145.

him from the mosque, even by dragging him by his hand or his foot, as deemed proper by the legists about every individual in whom an abominable smell is found by which people are offended. As for when one is not coming to the mosque, is it lawful to use [tobacco] just as it is lawful to eat onions and garlic, or not? There is no doubt that [tobacco] is not like onions and garlic, as both are among the things improving meals, and among the things constituting food for the poor, or what they eat with bread, whereas this tobacco is fundamentally not good for any of these [kinds of purposes].

F. 262r, l. 19, *qad kathura...* –> f. 263r, l. 10, *...iḥtiyāṭ*^{an} | L. 6, *qad kathura...* –> l. 51, *...iḥtiyāṭ*^{an}

Many things have been said about this [topic]. The truth on which to rely... –> ...out of precaution.

Main variants. – L. 15, *these three things*: *amusement, caprice and futility* **M**. L. 19, *And whatever the viewpoint from which it is looked at*: *Moreover* **M**. L. 33, *phlegmatic*: *phlegma* **M**. L. 37, *its users*: *those who have been using it* **M**. L. 39, *closest*: *due to the superabundance of their religiosity* + **M**. L. 41–42, *weakness in the body and heaviness in the limbs, covering in the vision and constipation in the digestive faculty. And this is because*: *covering in the vision and heaviness in the limbs, constipation in the digestive faculty and weakness in the body. It is indeed* **M**. L. 46–47, *leads to some harm*: *now, what leads to some harm, it is forbidden to use it*: – **M**.

F. 263r, l. 10, *thumma fī...* –> f. 263v, l. 19, *...al-muḥarram* | L. 58, *thumma inna...* –> l. 94, *...al-muḥarram*

In order to know whether things... –> ...under prodigality, which is prohibited.

Main variants. – L. 65–66, *there is no benevolence except by means of something useful and allowed*: *one is not benevolent except by means of something lawful and permitted* **M**. L. 70, *smoke, just smoke, in any respect*: *it* **M**. L. 74, *falls within what is prohibited, just as*: *is like* **M**. L. 75, *pasturing*: *falling* **M**. L. 91, *claim*: *say* **M**.

F. 263v, l. 19, *wa qad kataba...* –> f. 264r, l. 23, *...lam yaqbalū* | L. 120, *wa qad kataba...* –> l. 151, *...lā yaqbalūna*

In the Hijaz, some of the Mālikites have written... –> ...they do not accept it.

Main variants. – L. 121, *The use of*: – **M**. L. 126, *Jonah*: *the Prophet* + **M**. L. 131, *is a*: *painful* + **M**. L. 134, *a torment*: *it* **M**. L. 135, *their noses and their throats*: *their throats and their noses* **M**. L. 136, ḥadīth: *report* (khabar) **M**. L. 138, *two nostrils*: *nose* **M**. L. 142, *reported*: *established* **M**. L. 146–147, *using it had... Or, rather, if*: – **M**. L. 148, *with the purpose... be enough to*: *it would* **M**. L. 149, *engaging in it*: *Or, rather, if using it had no other* [*effect*] *than a blackening of the clothes and of the bodies, and the abomination of its smell and stink, it would hold back the intelligent individual from using it* + **M**. L. 150, *The natures of most of the people of this time are however rigid*: *Most of the people of this time are however* **M**.

F. 264r, l. 24, *wa in* – v, l. 1: Conclusion | —

If they are taught, they do not learn. If they are made to understand, they do not understand. If they understand, they amuse themselves with what they have understood. They are amongst those who, when they are shown the path of the right guidance, do not adopt it for path, whereas, when they are shown the path of misguidance, they adopt it for path. May God Most High make it easy for us to act in the manner appropriate to please Him, by His benevolence and generosity!

Majlis XCVII — *Dukhāniyyeh*

F. 264v, l. 1–9, *...wa l-ṣubyān*: Introduction ----

Council XCVII, making clear the obligation that one give up what should not concern him, either saying or action. – The Messenger of God – may God bless him and grant him peace – said: "The excellence of a person's *islām* consists, among other things, in giving up what should not concern him." This excellent *ḥadīth* of *al-Maṣābīḥ* is reported by Abū Hurayra. Its meaning is that a man's *islām* will not be perfect and excellent except when he gives up, in matter of sayings and actions, that in which there is fundamentally no usefulness for him, either in this life or in the hereafter. Now, among the things in which there is fundamentally no usefulness for him, is tobacco which, originating from the infidels, the enemies of the people of faith, has appeared in this time and by the inhalation (*maṣṣ*) of which the whole of mankind is afflicted, be it the elite or the commonalty. It appeared at the beginning of the eleventh century and became an enormous calamity (*fitna*) for the whole of humanity as its consumption spread, in [all] the countries, among men, women, and the young.

F. 264v, l. 9, *fa-lazima...* –> f. 266v, l. 5, *...wa akthar*	L. 5, *fa-wajaba...* –> l. 108, *...wa akthar*

It is thus compulsory on the ulema of the religion... —> ...being more intense and greater.

Main variants. – L. 14–15, *the prohibited character of these three things is known*: – hom. **M**. L. 31, *only*: – **M**. L. 42–43, *first and*: *and not* **M**. L. 49, *When the side of*: *When* **M**. L. 50, *numerous*: *many* **M**. L. 54, *whilst using it, are affected*: *are affected, when using it* **M**. L. 60–61, *a Legal proof*: *the Proof of the Law* **M**. L. 61, *a Legal proof*: *the Proof of the Law* **M**. L. 70, *smoke, just smoke, in any respect*: *it* **M**. L. 72, [*the*: *it is reported that* [*the* **M**. L. 75, *pasturing*: *falling* **M**. L. 86, *minimal*: *lowest* **M**. L. 87, *degree*: *rank* **M**. L. 88, *for every malady*: – **M**. L. 99–100, *the proof of this... one is offended*: – hom. **M**. L. 102, *in the mosque*: – **M**.

F. 266v, l. 5, *wa qad kataba...* –> f. 267r, l. 9, *...lam yaqbalū*	L. 120, *wa qad kataba...* –> l. 151, *...lā yaqbalūna*

In the Hijaz, some of the Mālikites have written... —> ...they do not accept it.

Main variants. – L. 126, *Jonah*: *the Prophet* + **M**. L. 128, *smoke*: – **M**. L. 130, *what is really meant by the* [*word*]: *real smoke* **M**. L. 131, *is a*: *painful* + **M**. L. 134, *and even more so*: a fortiori + **M**. L. 138, *it will come out*: – **M**.

F. 267r, l. 9, *wa in...* – l. 11: Conclusion —

If they are taught, they do not learn. If they are made to understand, they do not put into practice what they have understood. They are amongst those who, when they are shown the path of the right guidance, do not adopt it for path, whereas, when they are shown the path of misguidance, they adopt it for path.

"CHEATING ABOUT THE RELIGION OF GOD..."

THE Egyptian Mālikite shaykh Ibrāhīm al-Laqānī (d. 1041/1631) is more famous for his creed *The Jewel of Monotheism* (*Jawharat al-tawḥīd*) than for his treatise against smoking: *The Book Recommending to the Brothers to Keep Away from Tobacco* (*Kitāb naṣīḥat al-ikhwān bi-ijtināb al-dukhān*). The *Naṣīḥa*'s division into a prologue, an introduction, eleven chapters and a conclusion (*khātima*) should not mislead us: the work has nothing of the character of a formal study developing a clear argument and structuring its contents accordingly. It might just as well be regarded as a kind of literary souq or bazaar, with a colorful display of Indian drugs, narcotics and coffee as well as of tobacco, and a large assortment of explanations, warnings and anecdotes about the latter. Al-Laqānī's treatise is important however. Finished in Cairo in Rajab 1025 / July 1616, the *Naṣīḥa* is one of the very first Islamic works on tobacco. Also, al-Aqḥiṣārī's *Risāleh Dukhāniyyeh* appears to be directly related to it. In a marginal note appearing in each of the five manuscripts used for the preparation of this edition, al-Laqānī's name and the title of his *Naṣīḥa* explicitly accompany a passage borrowed from it.

One could of course argue that nothing proves that this note was added by al-Aqḥiṣārī himself. But what then must one say to explain the twenty-five or more passages of the *Dukhāniyyeh* in which he manifestly quotes or paraphrases, reuses or rewrites, parts of the *Naṣīḥa* and re-positions most of them, one vis-à-vis the other, according to his own agenda? Al-Aqḥiṣārī's debt to al-Laqānī is immense. The fact that he says nothing about it could be held against him and one may wonder what other sources he also drew upon. He should nevertheless be given credit for putting his borrowings to good use as he works out a far better conceived, and convincing, indictment against smoking than the Egyptian scholar. Somehow, one may even feel grateful to him. Indeed, a direct consequence of the obvious dependence of the *Dukhāniyyeh* on al-Laqānī's *Naṣīḥa* is that it is now possible to have some idea of the date when al-Aqḥiṣārī wrote his epistle and, also, published the *Majālis*, with its *Councils XCVI* and *XCVII* based on the *Dukhāniyyeh*: between Rajab 1025 / July 1616, date of the composition of the *Naṣīḥa* in Cairo, and the year himself passed away, i.e. 1041/1631 or 1043/1634.[1] Both the *Majālis* and the *Dukhāniyyeh* were thus composed during the years directly preceding, or corresponding to, the imperial ban on tobacco proclaimed by Murād IV after the great fire of Istanbul in 1043/1633.

Turkish Coffee-house[2]

Table of correspondences between the *Dukhāniyyeh* and al-Laqānī's *Naṣīḥa*

Dukhāniyyeh	***Naṣīḥa***
L. 21, *qāla*... –> l. 22, ...*'āmm*	Section VII, p. 42
L. 22, *wa qāla*... –> l. 24, ...*wa l-ḥammām*	Section VII, p. 40
L. 24, *wa dhukira*... –> l. 27, ...*kathīra*	Section VII, p. 42
L. 28, *wa qad*... –> ...*ḥarām*	Section VII, p. 41
L. 29, *fa-in*... –> l. 30, ...*aṣnāfi-hi*	Section VII, p. 43
L. 33, *fa-in qīla*... –> l. 35, ...*majhūl*	Conclusion, p. 72
L. 31, *anna-hum*... –> ...*yasīra*	Section VII, p. 43
L. 35, *fa-lā*... –> l. 37, ...*'adami-hā*	Section VII, p. 47
L. 37, *fa-in*... –> l. 43, ...*ākhir^{an}*	Section X, p. 52

1 The earliest of the 41 dated manuscripts of the *Majālis* that I have been able to examine at the Süleymaniye and Beyazıt Libraries in Istanbul and on the *yazmalar.gov.tr* website is Reşid Efendi 549, copied in 1044/1635.

2 *The Illustrated London News*, 3 December 1853, p. 468.

L. 44, *‘alā anna-hu… –>* l. 46, *…yuzīlu-hu*	Conclusion, p. 72
L. 58, *yarji‘u…–>* l. 66, *…al-mubāḥ*	Section XI, pp. 54–55
L. 67, *wa ‘alā… –>* l. 72, *…al-shar‘iyya*	Section XI, pp. 55–56
L. 72, *fa-inna-hu… –>* l. 76, *…ḥurmati-hā*	Conclusion, p. 60
L. 85, *fa-da‘…–>* l. 86, *…al-karāha*	Conclusion, pp. 60–61
L. 87, *wa lā… –> …al-ibāḥa*	Conclusion, p. 61
L. 88, *min… –>* l. 89, *…dawā’*	Section VII, p. 40
L. 90, *yalzamu… –>* l. 93, *…al-‘uqalā’*	Conclusion, p. 57
L. 94, *ma‘a… –>* l. 95, *…yasta‘milūna-hu*	Section VII, p. 44
L. 96, *wa qāla… –>* l. 98, *…bi-rīḥi-hi*	Section VII, p. 47
L. 109, *wa qad… –>* l. 118, *…jāmi‘*	Section VII, pp. 48–49
L. 120, *al-mālikiyya… –>* l. 129, *…alīm*	Conclusion, p. 71
L. 131, *al-fuqahā’… –>* l. 134, *…awlā*	Conclusion, p. 71
L. 135, *anna-hu… –>* l. 142, *…al-nār*	Conclusion, pp. 58–59
L. 143, *wa ṣaḥḥa… –>* l. 145, *…marra*	Conclusion, p. 59
L. 145, *fa-law… –>* l. 147, *…isti‘māli-hi*	Conclusion, p. 58
L. 147, *law lam… –>* l. 149, *…irtikābi-hi*	Conclusion, p. 60
L. 187, *yukhillu… –>* l. 188, *…‘adālati-hi*	Section VII, p. 45
L. 199, *al-qadr… –>* l. 210, *…maḍā*	Section I, pp. 31–32

F. Klein-Franke suggests that the author of *The Deliverance of Man from the Darknesses of Smoking* (*Risāla takhlīṣ al-insān ‘an ẓulumāt al-dukhān*), the Ḥanafite Medinese scholar ‘Abd al-Nāfi‘, “may have flourished at the end of the 16th century A.D.”[1] The beginning of the 11th/17th century is probably more correct. F. Klein-Franke has indeed not noticed that ‘Abd al-Nāfi‘ quotes verbatim a sentence of al-Aqḥiṣārī’s *Majālis*: “In the *Majālis* of al-Rūmī, [the author] says that when [the Prophet] – Peace be upon him – was finding on a man, in the mosque, a smell of onion or garlic, he used to give an order so that he was expelled to al-Baqī‘.”[2] We have just explained that the *Majālis* must be somewhat later than 1025/1616. This must necessarily also be the case for the *Takhlīṣ* of ‘Abd al-Nāfi‘. The ways in which the Medinese scholar and his Anatolian counterpart tackle the tobacco issue are very

1 F. Klein-Franke, *Smoking*, p. 157.

2 ‘Abd al-Nāfi‘, *Takhlīṣ*, p. 176, l. 125–126 = al-Aqḥiṣārī, *Majālis*, XCVI, f. 262r, l. 9–10 = XCVII, f. 266r, l. 23–24 = *Dukhāniyyeh*, l. 102–103.

different. ‘Abd al-Nāfi‘’s approach is essentially theological or, more precisely, exegetical. His purpose is to invalidate all apology for tobacco smoking on the basis of Qur’ān, *al-Baqara* – 2:29: “He it is Who created for you all that is on the earth.” In order to do so, his principal argument is another Qur’ānic verse, *al-A‘rāf* – 7:156: “He prohibits foul things (*khabā’ith*) to them.”[1] According to ‘Abd al-Nāfi‘, “foul things” are those that are found so by sound natural faculties and the smoke of tobacco is of course one of them. It is thus *ḥarām*. Some passages of the *Takhlīṣ* might remind the reader of views expressed by al-Aqḥiṣārī in his *Dukhāniyyeh*. Far more important to notice however is the fact that whereas ‘Abd al-Nāfi‘ condemns tobacco as foul, al-Aqḥiṣārī mainly refuses it because of its harmfulness (*maḍarra*) and its offensive character. Rather than being determined by scriptural aesthetics, the Anatolian scholar’s ethics is thus pragmatic. Because of the authority that he accords to medicine and his concern for others as well as, more generally, for social realities, his religiosity might even be considered, in some way, as much profane as it is theological and, hence, less traditional than pre-modern. Puritanism does not necessarily entail a purely medieval mindset…

The Palestinian shaykh Mar‘ī b. Yūsuf al-Karmī (d. in Cairo, 1033/1623) is a surprising character. Ḥanbalite, biographer and admirer of Ibn Taymiyya, he might have been expected to find some Qur’ānic verse or Prophetic tradition that could, so as to prohibit tobacco, play the role of one of those “comprehensive words” with which the Prophet has been sent; i.e. words of “general interest, concerning all that is covered by their formulation and meaning, whether the concrete things [discussed] existed or not in the [Prophet’s] time, or at the place where he was.”[2] In order to prohibit cannabis, Ibn Taymiyya had for example underlined the “comprehensive words” quality of the *ḥadīth* “Everything inebriating is wine and all wine is prohibited.” In his *Determination of the Real Proof on the Matter of Tobacco – Taḥqīq al-burhān fī*

1 For a detailed modern demonstration of the prohibited nature of tobacco based on its foul essence and this verse 7:156, see S. Nadā, quoted in the introduction of M. al-Karmī, *Taḥqīq*, pp. 78–81.

2 Ibn Taymiyya, *MF*, trans. Michot, *Haschich*, p. 82.

sha'n al-dukhān, al-Karmī accepts that "every authorized thing distracting from something obligatory is religiously prohibited (*ḥarām*)." Quoting Ibn Taymiyya, he moreover condemns as *ḥarām* the vicious, immoderate, excessive way in which tobacco is collectively smoked in his time, notably because of its harmfulness for families, and invites his readers to keep away from such smokers.[1] Nevertheless, he considers neither this general rule nor these circumstances as relevant or sufficient to prohibit smoking *per se*.[2] As for those claiming that if tobacco had appeared in the time of the Prophet he would have prohibited it, he makes a butt of their pretention to know the unknowable (*ghayb*).[3] He acknowledges the abominable nature of the odour of tobacco smoke, likens smokers to the inhabitants of hell, denounces the futility of smoking and the waste of money it entails but refuses to call it religiously prohibited (*ḥarām*), out of fear of exceeding God's limits.[4] Rather than rushing into an illegitimate prohibition on the basis of personal opinion (*ra'y*) and preference (*istiḥsān*), he favours the ponderation of Ibn Ḥanbal and the strict literalism of Ibn Ḥazm.[5] Perhaps with 'Abd al-Nāfi' in mind, he finds amazing that some jurists base their prohibition of tobacco on its supposedly "foul" nature (*khubth*).[6] For him, the case of tobacco is in fact similar to that of coffee, hastily prohibited by some jurists when it appeared but "about the lawfulness of which there is now, in this time, a consensus (*ijmā'*)",[7] and he is not ready to go further than declaring smoking detested (*makrūh*).[8] The insistence shown and the juristic maestria deployed by al-Karmī against prohibiting smoking *per se* are all the more impressive as he regarded it as a personal vice and a repugnant collective practice. One therefore cannot help wondering what game he was really playing. In comparison,

1 M. al-Karmī, *Taḥqīq*, pp. 109–111.
2 M. al-Karmī, *Taḥqīq*, p. 144.
3 M. al-Karmī, *Taḥqīq*, pp. 140–141.
4 M. al-Karmī, *Taḥqīq*, pp. 115, 147, 127, 156.
5 M. al-Karmī, *Taḥqīq*, pp. 143, 132–133.
6 M. al-Karmī, *Taḥqīq*, p. 139.
7 M. al-Karmī, *Taḥqīq*, pp. 152–155.
8 M. al-Karmī, *Taḥqīq*, pp. 127, 131.

al-Aqḥiṣārī's argumentation appears, from the standpoint of technical juristic sophistication, a good deal less impressive. Nevertheless, one is tempted to think that his whole approach to the issue was more faithful to Ibn Taymiyya's puritanical societal reformism than the *ẓāhirī* ratiocinations of the latter's so-called disciple.

[1]

When Kātib Çelebi, in 1067/1656, completes his *Balance of Truth* (*Mīzān al-ḥaqq*), the vicissitudes suffered by tobacco after its introduction into Turkey have come to an end and smoking is openly practised in most Ottoman milieus. A few years earlier the Sheykhülislām Bahā'ī Efendi, "a man of right nature and sound sense", issued a fatwā ruling that it was lawful, "not out of regard for his own addiction (*ibtilā'*) but because he considered what was best suited to the condition of the people and because he held fast to the principle that permissibility (*ibāḥat*) is the norm."[2] In Chapter V – *Tobacco* – of his book, Kātib Çelebi remembers former times, when "the great doctors of the law (*mashāyikh-e islām*) have [...] pronounced it disapproved (*karāhat*), in the greater interest of the public (*maṣlaḥat*) while certain provincial muftis (*kenār muftīleri*) have declared it forbidden (*ḥurmat*)."[3] We will never know who exactly the Ottoman intellectual meant by these prohibitionist "provincial", or "marginal" (*kenār*), muftis. Most probably the Qāḍīzādelis, partisans indeed of a total proscription of both tobacco and coffee and in whom Murād IV, whilst being influenced by

1 Drawings in E. R. Billings, *Tobacco*, pp. 363, 370.

2 Kātib Çelebi, *Mīzān*, p. 206, trans. Lewis, *Balance*, pp. 56–57.

3 Kātib Çelebi, *Mīzān*, p. 206, trans. Lewis, *Balance*, p. 56 (with a correction).

them,[1] had found the most complacent allies of his despotic prohibition of the two substances. Possibly, also, the Anatolian scholar Aḥmad al-Rūmī al-Aqḥiṣārī, himself a strict prohibitionist of the Qāḍīzādeli type as obvious from his *Dukhāniyyeh* or *Majālis*, and who was surely known to Kātib Çelebi, as the latter writes of his having been the teacher of al-Aqḥiṣārī's son Mevlānā Meḥmed in 1057/1647.[2]

A Street in Constantinople[3]

As tobacco addiction spread uncontrollably amongst Ottomans, the failure of puritanical reformists like al-Aqḥiṣārī soon appeared total[4] in

1 See S. Çavuşoğlu, *Movement*, pp. 217–218.

2 Kātib Çelebi, *Mīzān*, trans. Lewis, *Balance*, p. 142.

3 *Le Magasin Pittoresque*, vol. viii (Paris, 1840), p. 237.

4 Al-Aqḥiṣārī's prohibitionist views on tobacco nevertheless influenced various Ottoman authors. The quotation of a sentence of the *Majālis* by the Medinese ʿAbd al-Nāfiʿ has already been noted *supra* (p. 36). In *Movement*, p. 221, S. Çavuşoğlu refers to an anonymous *Risāle-i Dukhāniye* (MS. *Süleymaniye, Erzincan* 144/3) whose author "states that according to Şeykh A ḥmed Rūmī el-Aḳḥisārī *şeykhül-*

Turkey and the "provincial muftis" of Kātib Çelebi sometimes became the object of the most injurious insults. In his *Epistle on the authorized nature of tobacco* (*Risāla fī ibāḥat al-dukhān*), the Syrian Sufi master 'Abd al-Ghanī al-Nābulusī (d. 1143/1731) writes for example about the prohibitionists of tobacco: "The conditions of this time are changed by its ignoramuses, who command and forbid things about which they haven't got a clue. They call themselves ascetics and advisers, and see others neither as Muslims nor as virtuous. They say with their tongues things that are not in their hearts. They adorn their faces with the opposite of what is in their bosoms. They spy on the failings of people night and day. They admonish the ulema in private and in public. They call people unbelievers for petty reasons. They impose restrictions on the masses without proof. They prohibit and declare lawful what they want. They are the ones leading astray, followed by the misled. They are, inwardly, foxes and, outwardly, sheep. They employ artful means to gather this world's wealth as if they were plundering it. They want but to be seen of men yet refuse [them] the necessaries of life. They are cursing and causing much hurt, just as the plague does. They do not want the Raghā'ib prayers in any oratory and prevent the servant from praying. To enforce their policies of corruption, they join all together and they think that they are doing something excellent. They are content with the acts of disobedience of those who are like them and displeased with the good deeds of the others. They are hinderers of good and go about with slanders, detracting and defaming in every ignoble manner, regretful when an opportunity to express some of the wickedness which they conceal in their hearts has been missed, serving the pigs of lust and the dogs of the self. When the people of truth give them some sincere advice, they do not follow it. Deaf, dumb and blind, they do not reason. They appeal for justice but are not just. They cheat about the religion of God out of stubbornness and treat the creatures of God haughtily out of wickedness. Woe unto them and those who have led them astray, unto those who follow them and revere them. With God we seek refuge and

islām Ebūssu'ūd Efendi gave a *fetvā* for the illegality of coffee." This is effectively the case in al-Aqḥiṣārī's *Dukhāniyyeh*, l. 193–198. This influence remains to be studied systematically.

take shelter against their evils. May God protect our brothers from their deception."[1]

Istanbul 2008: the end of an epoch

In 2008, the Turkish Law No. 5727 finally brought some sort of concession to al-Aqḥiṣārī and other Ottoman prohibitionists of smoking. That this vindication of past "fundamentalist" reformists against their supposedly more "enlightened" opponents proceeds from the policies of a modern state should only seem paradoxical to people with a poor understanding of the societal concerns and ideals of such Muslim puritans. As S. Çavuşoğlu rightly remarks, "the Qāḍīzādeli movement is at least partially to be understood as a reform-oriented response to a perceived decadence in the Ottoman order in the seventeenth century."[2]

* * *

THE present edition and translation of al-Aqḥiṣārī's *Epistle on Tobacco* are based on five manuscripts from Turkey:[3]

1 'A. Gh. al-Nābulusī, *Ibāḥa*, p. 2.

2 S. Çavuşoğlu, *Movement*, p. 66.

3 MS. *Giresun 114* (p. 27 right–left of the digital copy of the Süleymaniye Library's computer) contains only a passage of the epistle (l. 178–198 of our edition). A. Āl Salmān (introd. of M. al-Karmī, *Taḥqīq*, p. 99, no 42) mentions the MS. Damascus, *Dār al-Kutub al-Ẓāhiriyya 5410*, which I was unable to use for this edition.

A: Manisa, *İl Halk Kütüphanesi*, *Akhisar Zeynelzade Koleksiyon*, 45 Ak Ze 1602/1, ff. 1v–6r. Collection (*majmūʻa*) including five epistles of al-Aqḥiṣārī. No date (12th/18th century?). Cursive *naskh* script. A few interlinear and marginal corrections. F. 1r, a note in the left superior corner reads: "This noble epistle which makes clear the unpermissibility to use [tobacco-]smoking is by the learned and eminent shaykh and hadji Aḥmad al-Aqḥiṣārī – may God Most High protect him from [all] harms and infirmities in the two realms. Amen! O You Who answer those who ask!"[1]

D: *Darülmesnevi 258*, ff. 70v–74v. *Majmūʻa* including seven epistles of al-Aqḥiṣārī. Ff. 109v, 143r, colophons date this manuscript to Shaʻbān 1093, i.e. August 1682. Cursive but regular and clear *naskh* script. A few marginal notes. F. 143r, a marginal note attributes the *Epistle refuting al-Ṣaghānī* (see *supra*, p. 6, no 3) to "the eminent shaykh Aḥmad al-Rūmī the Ḥanafite, who resided a while in the city (*qaṣaba*) of Aqḥiṣār". F. 70v, the *Epistle on Tobacco* is called *Risāleh dukhāniyyeh*.

H: *Harput 429*, ff. 194v–199v. An important *majmūʻa* of 200 folios devoted to al-Aqḥiṣārī and comprising nineteen epistles. F. 1r, the deed of endowment (*waqf*) is dated 1246[/1830]. The manuscript does not seem much older: 12th/18th century? Regular and clear *naskh* script. Several marginal corrections and notes. In the table of contents (*fihrist*) of the manuscript, f. 1r, the *Epistle on Tobacco* is called *Risāleh dukhāniyyeh*.

K: *Kılıç Ali Paşa 1035*, ff. 31v–36v. *Majmūʻa* including seven epistles of al-Aqḥiṣārī. F. 69r, a colophon is dated 1036[/1624] but the

1 The text which appears under the title *Dukhāniyyeh – On tobacco*, ff. 93v–95v of this same MS. Manisa İHK, *Akhisar Zeynelzade Koleksiyon*, 45 Ak Ze 1602/7, is a shorter epistle than the *Risāleh dukhāniyyeh*. Explicitly attributed to "the shaykh Aḥmad al-Aqḥiṣārī" (f. 93r), it aims to demonstrate that smoking tobacco breaks the fast of Ramaḍān, it includes passages corresponding to ll. 2–3, 6–14, 14–16, 19–27, 33–51, 58–76, 83–90, 94–98, 101–105, 120–129, 131–145 of this edition of the *Risāleh dukhāniyyeh*, sometimes in a version closer to that of *Council XCVI* of the *Majālis*. It also includes a reference to the Muʻtazilites, present in al-Laqānī's *Naṣīḥa*, p. 58, but absent from the *Risāleh dukhāniyyeh* and *Council XCVI*.

manuscript seems more recent: early 12th/18th century? Clear little *nasta'līq* script. Several marginal corrections and notes. The *Epistle on Tobacco* has no title (and is not identified in the Süleymaniye Library's computer).

R: *Reisülküttab 1182* (*1181*), ff. 52v–57r. *Majmūʻa* including four epistles of al-Aqḥiṣārī. No date is given: 11th/17th century? Irregular cursive *nasta'līq* script. Several notes in Arabic and in Turkish are added in the margins, as well as a number of short fatwās concerning tobacco, coffee, opium and other drugs. Some will be translated in the footnotes of our translation. F. 52v, in the margin, the *Epistle on Tobacco* is given the title *Risāleh el-Taʻaṣṣubiyyeh – Epistle of Bigotry*.

Although it is not the oldest copy, MS. **H** was preferred to the four others because it is written in a particularly clear and regular *naskh*. It is its foliation which is indicated in square brackets in the edition. Several obvious mistakes that it contains were corrected by collating it with MSS. **ADKR**. These emendations are reported in the footnotes of the edition. The various mistakes and insignificant variants of MSS. **ADKR** are not signalled. In one instance, a correction is suggested on the basis of al-Laqānī's *Naṣīḥa* (**N**), in a passage of the latter quoted by al-Aqḥiṣārī. The punctuation and layout into paragraphs are mine.

In relation to classical Arabic, al-Aqḥiṣārī's language suffers from several imperfections which are not corrected in the edition. Our editing of his text was limited to keeping the writing of the *hamza*s and of some words in conformity with modern conventions (*ṣalāt* rather than *ṣal*^{w}*at*; *thalātha* rather than *thalatha*), as well as to supplying *shadda*s and some vocalization, where deemed useful for a clear understanding of the text.

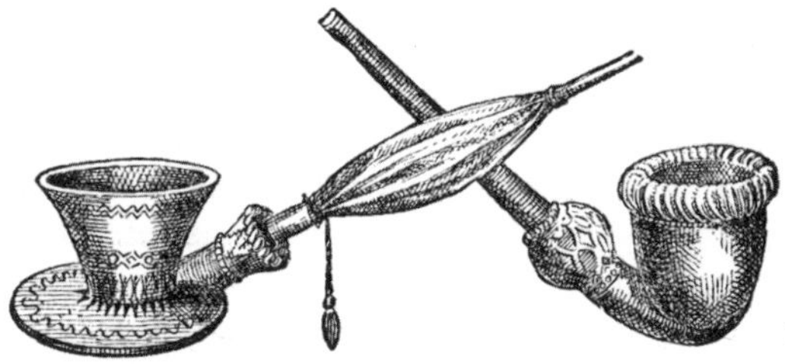
[1]

[1] Turkish pipes. Drawing in E. R. Billings, *Tobacco*, p. 172.

Translation

In the Name of God, the Merciful, the Compassionate

ALL praise is due to God! Blessing and peace be upon the Messenger of God and upon the family of the Messenger of God!

Originating from the infidels, the enemies of the people of faith, the leaf of a plant has appeared in this time which is called "tobacco" (*dukhān*)[1] and by the inhalation (*shurb*) of the smoke of which the whole of mankind is afflicted, be it the elite or the commonalty. **[5]** It is thus obligatory on the ulema of the religion to make clear its status to the Muslims: is it lawful to use it or is it obligatory to keep away from it? Listen then, O you men of sound minds, to what will be said to you on this topic about which many things are said.

The truth on which to rely is that if no advantage – religious or worldly – derives from the [freely] chosen (*ikhtiyārī*) action emanating from a Legally responsible person (*mukallaf*), such an action oscillates between futility (*ʻabath*), amusement (*laʻib*) and caprice (*lahw*). In **[10]** the dictionaries (*kitāb al-lugha*), no difference is made between these three things. Nevertheless, unavoidably, there must be a difference since, in the Qur'ān, they are attached to one another by conjunctions.[2] The fact is indeed – as one of scholarship's stallions (*faḥl*) has mentioned it,[3] and it is what deserves to be received favourably – that [by]

1 *Dukhān* is the only term used for tobacco in this epistle. I. al-Laqānī (*Naṣīḥa*, Section vii, p. 38) mentions several other words used by the common people (*ʻāmma*): *tubbāk*, *tutun*, *tabgha*, *ṭābgha*.

2 *ʻAbath* appears only once in the Qur'ān, without any connection to the two other terms: "Did you then think that We had created you futilely (*ʻabath^{an}*)?" (Qur'ān, *al-Mu'minūn* - 23:115). As for *laʻib* and *lahw*, they indeed appear joined together by a *wa* in several Qur'ānic verses, for example, *al-Anʻām* - 6:32: "And this world's life is naught but amusement and caprice."

3 In a passage on the same subject of his *Epistle on the prohibition of dancing and whirling* (*Raqṣ*, MS. Istanbul, *Harput 429*, f. 65r; see *supra*, p. 8, no 15), al-

futility is [meant] an action in which there is neither pleasure nor advantage. As for an action in which there is pleasure without advantage, it is [called] *amusement*. Similar to it is *caprice*, except that the soul is more involved in the latter, so that it becomes distracted thereby from what should concern it. These things are all prohibited (*ḥarām*) since, in the Qur'ān, they are not mentioned except in a blameworthy way. As the prohibited character of these three things is known, the prohibited character of the use of this tobacco also becomes known, as it is subsumed under either amusement, or caprice, or futility. Or rather, it pertains more to futility as it is devoid of the pleasure that there is in amusement and caprice. My God, [it must be so] unless the souls of some of those who use it find it pleasurable because of some satanic enticement! In which case it is subsumed under amusement or caprice.

And whatever the viewpoint from which it is looked at, it is void of religious advantage – which is obvious – as well as of worldly advantage, since it is fundamentally suitable neither as food nor as medicine. On the contrary, it is harmful, as the physicians are agreed on the fact that smoke, just smoke, in all respects, is harmful. "If there were no smoke and darkness (*qatām*)," Avicenna has said, "the son of Adam would live a thousand years!" Also, Galen has said: "Keep away from three things, make an obligation of four, and you will have no need for the doctor! Keep away from smoke, dust, and putrescence; make an obligation of [eating] fatty foods and [eating] sweet things, perfuming and bathing." In the *Canon*, it is stated that all the sorts of smoke are dessicating, due to their earthy substance and because there is, in them, a slight igneousness.[1] As all sorts of smoke are dessicating, one of

Aqḥiṣārī mentions explicitly the name of this "stallion of scholarship": "al-Ḥaddādī", i.e. Abū Bakr b. 'Alī al-Ḥaddād(ī) l-'Abbādī al-Yamanī (d. 800/1397), author of *al-Sirāj al-wahhāj – The Shining Lamp*, commentary on one of the most famous manuals of applied Ḥanafite law, *al-Mukhtaṣar* of al-Qudūrī; see G. Brockelmann, *GAL*, vol. i, p. 183, no 12; A. Özel, *Alimleri*, p. 94; Y. Michot, *Opium*, p. 98 (where the date 880/1397 must be corrected to 800/1397).

1 See Ibn Sīnā, *Qānūn*, vol. i, p. 476: "All the sorts of smoke are dessicating, due to their earthy substance and because there is, in them, a slight igneousness (*yasīr nāriyya*)."

the eminent [scholars][1] has said, this [tobacco] smoke will be dessicating the bodily humours and thereby leading to the occurrence of many sicknesses. It is therefore not permitted to use it, due to the obligation to protect oneself from being touched by harms. In the *Niṣāb al-iḥtisāb*,[2] it is indeed stated that using something harmful is prohibited.

Smokers[3]

"Some physicians might treat some sicknesses by means of some sorts of smoke, **[30]** whose usefulness is thus observed. How would it therefore be valid to forbid using all its sorts?" If this is said, the answer will be that they only treat thereby [a patient] during a short moment, not permanently, so that the dessication mentioned obtains [for that short moment].

1 Probably I. al-Laqānī, freely quoted here (*Naṣīḥa*, Section vii, p. 42).

2 Work by the Ḥanafite jurist ʿUmar b. Muḥammad b. ʿIwaḍ al-Sunnāmī (d. 696/1297); see G. Brockelmann, *GAL*, *Suppl.*, vol. ii, p. 427. I. al-Laqānī (*Naṣīḥa*, Section vii, p. 41) gives a more precise reference: "Section xxxvi of the *Niṣāb al-iḥtisāb*".

3 Left: Detail from postcard, Constantinople, Max Fruchtermann, no 105, *c.* 1900. Right: Anonymous, Yenidjé cigarette paper advert, Turkey, *c.* 1910.

"The dessication that has been mentioned does not harm the phlegmatic [subject] due to the abundance of his humours and the fact that he benefits from having them dessicated. What then is the point in forbidding this [tobacco] smoke?" If this is said, the answer will be that the extent to which one benefits from it is **[35]** unknown. In order to know that, one unavoidably needs a physician, [one] expert and knowledgeable about the complexions as well as of the measure in which one would benefit from it. Otherwise, to venture therein is absolutely prohibited, because of the real uncertainty concerning its safeness or unsafeness. Indeed, the persons of probity (*'adl*), among its users, have differed in opinion about it. Among them, there are some who speak of its harmfulness, some who speak of its absence of harmfulness and some who entertain doubts on the matter. The most numerous group, from whom the side of truth is the closest, however, says that, in the beginning, it produces strength in the body and sharpness in **[40]** the vision, ardour in the limbs and [good] digestion during a meal. When one comes to use it permanently, however, it causes weakness in the body and heaviness in the limbs, covering in the vision and constipation in the digestive faculty. And this [is] because it is, as stated by the physicians, dessicating with a kind of heat. In the beginning, it thus does what they mentioned first and, in the end, what they mentioned last.

And even if its usefulness turned out to be true, after being useful it would still be forbidden to use it because, in that case, it would be a medicine. **[45]** Now, it is not permitted to use a medicine after the sickness has ceased because, if it does not find a sickness that it might cause to cease, it starts on the body and leads to some harm; now, what leads to some harm, it is forbidden to use it. Does one not see that the Qur'ān has informed us of the usefulness of wine, which is nevertheless textually prohibited? Thus did God Most High say: "They question you concerning wine and gambling. Say: "In both is great sin, and [some] utility for men."[1] When the side of harmfulness stands exactly opposite to the side of usefulness, the side of harmfulness covers [it] however. "If **[50]** in something," the jurists have consequently said, "there are

[1] Qur'ān, *al-Baqara* - 2:219.

numerous aspects necessitating lawfulness and permissibility (*jawāz*), and one aspect necessitating prohibition and absence of permissibility, the side of prohibition shall preponderate, out of precaution."[1]

"Those who use it claim that, after using it, they feel a lightness in their body. How then would it be valid to speak of an absence of usefulness in regard to it?" If this is said, the answer will be – according to what has been mentioned by some of those who have consumed it in order to experience its usefulness and its harmfulness – that those who use it, whilst using it, **[55]** are affected by an intense pain and, once they are rid of it, are delivered from such a pain, whilst tranquillity (*rāḥa*) befalls them. These poor folk think that such a tranquillity results from using it and do not know that it only results from being freed from its use.

In order to know whether things are prohibited or allowed (*ibāḥa*), there is also an excellent approach that will take us back to the principles. It is that the truth concerning things, before the sending [of the Prophet], was that they did not have a status (*ḥukm*), and that after the sending [of the Prophet] **[60]** the ulema, whilst differing about them, have said three things. The first is that things are to be described as prohibited, except what a Legal proof proves to be allowed. The second is that they are to be described as allowed, except what a Legal proof proves to be prohibited. The third, which is the valid [position], is that some classification is to be introduced about them; i.e. the harmful things are to be described as prohibited in the sense that the principle, in them, is to be prohibited, whereas the useful things are to be described as allowed in the sense that the principle, in them, is to be allowed, since the Most High has said: "He it is Who created for you **[65]** all that is on the earth."[2] Now, He stated this – Most High is He – as a display

1 Al-Karmī (*Taḥqīq*, pp. 134–135) defends the opposite view: "Tobacco is pure and devoid of harmfulness with a balanced complexion—the people of experience are agreed on this. It is thus lawful, and one should not pay attention to an individual to whom, because of it, something happens which harms him."

2 Qur'ān, *al-Baqara* - 2:29. On the use of this verse in favour of tobacco or against it, see F. Klein-Franke, *Smoking*, pp. 159–161; ʿAbd al-Nāfiʿ, *Takhlīṣ*, pp. 172–174.

of benevolence, and there is no benevolence except by means of something useful and allowed. It is therefore as if the Most High had said: "He it is Who created for your sake all that which, in respect of useful things, is on the earth, so that you might benefit from them." It is also on the basis of this third, valid, saying that the status of this [tobacco] smoke will be deduced.

PUNISHMENT FOR SNUFF-TAKING.

"Gradually His Majesty's severity in suppression increased, and so did people's desire to smoke, in accordance with the saying, 'Men desire what is forbidden'..."[1]

If indeed it was useful, the principle, in it, would be that it is allowed. It is however established by the reports of **[70]** the most skilled of the physicians that smoke, just smoke, in any respect, is harmful, be it only

[1] Kātib Çelebi, *Mīzān*, trans. Lewis, *Balance*, p. 51. Drawing in E. R. Billings, *Tobacco*, p. 104.

in the long term. The principle in it shall thus be that it is prohibited. And even if there was some doubt about the matter, the side of prohibition would still prevail, as asserted by the Legal rule. [The Prophet] has indeed said, blessing and peace be upon him: "What is lawful is clear, what is prohibited is clear and, between the two, there are unclear things that are not known by many people. Someone fearing these unclear things preserves his religion and his honour whereas someone falling in these unclear things falls within what is prohibited, just as a shepherd grazing [his flocks] around a sanctuary (*ḥimā*) **[75]** is on the point of pasturing in it."[1]

The ulema have differed in opinion about the status of these unclear things. Some of them have held the view that it is to be prohibited because [the Prophet], blessing and peace be upon him, has informed us in this *ḥadīth* that the religion of someone abstaining from a thing whose status is unclear for him and the reality of whose affair is not disclosed to him is safe from what might corrupt it or make it deficient whilst his soul escapes what would blemish it and cause it to be blamed; whereas someone not abstaining from it but, on the contrary, doing it, will fall into what is prohibited. Now, this [tobacco] smoke is among the things whose status **[80]** is unclear and the reality of whose affair has not been disclosed. The religion of someone abstaining from it and not using it is thus safe from corruption and deficiency whilst his soul escapes being blemished and blamed among people; whereas someone not abstaining from it but, on the contrary, using it, will fall into what is prohibited.

As for others, they have held the view that it is to be detested (*karāha*) because it is mentioned in another *ḥadīth* that [the Prophet], blessing and peace be upon him, had said: "Affairs are of three [sorts]: an affair whose well guided character is clear to you; so, follow it! an affair whose straying character is clear to you; **[85]** so, keep away from it! an affair about which there are divergences; so, leave what will fill

[1] See al-Bukhārī, *Ṣaḥīḥ*, vol. i, p. 20; Muslim, *Ṣaḥīḥ*, vol. v, pp. 50–51; Ibn Ḥanbal, *Musnad*, vol. iv, p. 269.

you with suspicion in favour of what will not fill you with suspicion!"[1] Now, there is no doubt that the affair of [tobacco] smoke is among the things that fill one with suspicion and make him fall into confusion. The minimal rank [to attribute to] it shall thus be: to be detested.

And let us not be of the opinion that it would end up at the degree of being allowed for the reason that many of those who indulge in it allege that it is useful, that it is a remedy for every malady,[2] and that, in using it, they have found a remedy to their sicknesses. This indeed results from the devil deceiving them and adorning it in their [mind] with such qualities that, in the end, [for them], nothing else is generated from the density of its [inhalation] than a remedy. [Using] it repeatedly however **[90]** makes something predominate that is its opposite and from which heat is generated, so that, in the end, there is a sickness, not a remedy. Moreover, from what they claim, it would necessarily follow that people are all sick, that their sickness would be of one same species during each of the four seasons, and that curing them from it would be by means of the one same thing, in the one same manner! Now, the falsity of such an [affirmation] is hidden to none of the intelligent people!

In [smoking tobacco], there is also a waste of one's wealth as it is bought at an expensive price. It thus falls under prodigality (*isrāf*), which is prohibited.[3] Not to speak of **[95]** the stinking of its smell and of its obnoxiousness for those who breathe it without using it! In the *ḥadīth*, it is stated: "Every obnoxious individual will be in the Fire."[4] "A

[1] This "*ḥadīth*" is in fact made up of two traditions. First, a saying attributed to Jesus by the Prophet and not found in the six canonic *ḥadīth* collections "*Affairs are of three* [*sorts*] *only: an affair… divergences; so*, take it back to the person who knows it!" (see al-Haythamī, *Majma'*, vol. i, p. 157). Second, "What is prohibited is clear, what is lawful is clear and, in between, there are unclear matters. *So, leave what will fill you with suspicion in favour of what will not fill you with suspicion!*" (see al-Dārimī, *Sunan*, vol. i, p. 61; al-Nasā'ī, *Sunan*, vol. viii, p. 231).

[2] For an example of a text extolling tobacco as a universal medicine, see F. Klein-Franke, *Smoking*, p. 157.

[3] Prodigality is prohibited in various verses of the Qur'ān, for example in *al-An'ām* - 6:141: "Be not prodigal. Lo! God loves not the prodigal."

[4] This tradition, often reported from 'Alī, is not in the six canonic *ḥadīth* collections. Ibn Kathīr quotes it in his *Tafsīr* (vol. i, p. 59) on the authority of al-Qurṭubī: "In

stinking smell," al-Miknāsī[1] has said, "pierces the nose, reaches the brain and is noxious to man." The Prophet, blessing and peace be upon him, therefore said: "Whoever eats of this plant shall not at all come near to our mosque, offending us with his smell!"[2] What is meant by "this plant" is the [whole] genus of that which has an abominable smell by which one is offended, the proof of this being that he, blessing and peace be upon him, gave a justification for his [decision]. **[100]** The meaning [of this *ḥadīth*] is: "Someone eating anything having an abominable smell by which one is offended shall not at all come near to our mosque because he would offend us with its abominable smell." In the *Ṣaḥīḥ* of Muslim,[3] it is established that when [the Prophet], blessing and peace be upon him, was finding on a man, in the mosque, a smell of onion or garlic, he used to give an order so that he was expelled to al-Baqī'.[4] "Every individual," the jurists have therefore said, "on whom an

the *ḥadīth*, it is reported about the Prophet, blessing and peace be upon him, that he said: "Every obnoxious individual will be in the Fire". This *ḥadīth* is neither [canonically] preserved nor well known."

1 'Abd al-'Azīz b. 'Abd al-'Azīz al-Lamaṭī l-Miknāsī l-Maymūnī (d. *c.* 880/1475), Maghrebi Mālikite jurist and grammarian; see Kh. D. al-Ziriklī, *A'lām*, vol. iv, p. 21. I. al-Laqānī (*Naṣīḥa*, Section vii, p. 47), whom al-Aqḥiṣārī is quoting here, gives a more precise reference: "al-Miknāsī, in [his] *Marginal Comments* (*Ḥawāshī*) on the *Compendium* (*Mukhtaṣar*) of Khalīl, in the chapter *On Association*".

2 Several versions exist of this tradition. See notably Muslim, *Ṣaḥīḥ*, vol. ii, p. 79; Abū Dā'ūd, *Sunan*, vol. iii, p. 361, no 3825. In another version, this *ḥadīth* also speaks of the angels being offended by abominable smells. Al-Aqḥiṣārī quotes it in the introduction of his *Majlis* XCVI, translated *supra*, but not in the *Dukhāniyyeh*. Here, he exclusively speaks of smoking as annoying humans, in contradistinction to al-Azharī (*Ḥukm*, p. 186), who makes offending the angels an important element of his argumentation against tobacco.

3 See Muslim, *Ṣaḥīḥ*, vol. ii, p. 81.

4 A desolate field in Medina, originally covered with a kind of bramble, which became the first Islamic cemetery of the city; see A. J. Wensinck & A. S. Bazmee Ansari, *EI2*, art. *Baḳī' al-Gharḳad*.

"The status of someone who exhales an abominable smell, like bad breath, etc.," people have said, "is also the status of the individual eating of these two plants" [i.e. onion and garlic]. "Someone having bad breath or a wound that smells," some of them have said, "shall be treated like him." "The members of [our] legal school treat like that – i.e. the individual eating garlic, etc. – people employed in mal-

abominable smell is found by which one is offended, it is obligatory to expel him from the mosque, even by dragging him by his hand and his foot – but not by his beard or the hair of **[105]** his head. In this time, it is consequently obligatory to expel from the mosques – the small ones (*masjid*) and the great ones (*jāmi'*) – many of the imāms and muezzins on whom there is an abominable smell because of their constant use of this [tobacco] smoke with its abominable smell. Sometimes, they even use it inside the mosques, small and great; the abomination, in that case, being more intense and greater.[1]

Ce vieil homme, qui fumait beaucoup et parlait peu, était *muezzin,* chargé de chanter, matin et soir, la prière musulmane.

"Smoking like Turks…»[2]

odorous professions, like fishmongers and butchers" (MS. **R**, f. 54v, marginal notes).

1 In two requests for a fatwā adressed to the Sheykhülislām Yaḥyā Efendi (d. 1053 /1644), one reads: "When tobacco-smokers arrive at the mosques, Muslims are annoyed because of the bad smell of their mouth and their garments…" "If some townspeople come to the mosque smoking with tobacco pipes in their hands, how should they be treated according to the *şerī'at*?" (trans. S. Çavuşoğlu, *Movement*, pp. 240–241).

2 Left: drawing by J. P. Pinchon, *Becassine*, p. 15. Right: advert in *The Saturday Evening Post*, June 5, 1915, p. 48.

From one of those afflicted by [smoking], it is reported that he used to say: “It is lawful. If it was not, **[110]** onions, garlic and leeks would also be prohibited!” Such words, on his part, are vain because the [Prophetic] text concerning these [vegetables] does not indicate anything else than the interdiction, for someone eating them, to come near to the mosque only, as it would necessarily follow therefrom that they would offend the Muslims with their smell, when coming near to the mosque and attending the collective prayer. As for someone eating them and not coming near to the mosque, the [Prophetic] text is silent about him. What it establishes is only the lawfulness of eating them without coming near to the mosque, as the Prophet, blessing and peace be upon him, acknowledged their eating. If not, he would have forbidden it just as he forbade [one eating them] to come near to the mosque.[1] Not to mention the fact that there is a difference **[115]** between these [vegetables] and [tobacco] smoke: they are among the things improving meals and constituting food for the poor, or what they eat with bread, just as was the case during the raid on Khaybar, during which garlic and leeks provided the core of what the [Muslims] took as nourishment, to the point that the corners of their mouths were ulcered.[2] Now, this [tobacco] smoke is not like this, as it is fundamentally not good for any of these [purposes]. The analogy (*qiyās*) [put forward as an argument] is thus of a corrupt nature as it is an analogical syllogism (*qiyās*) without anything joining [its two elements].

1 See Muslim, *Ṣaḥīḥ*, vol. ii, p. 80: when the Prophet forbade Companions who had eaten garlic to come near to him in the mosque, “people said: “[Garlic] has been prohibited! It has been prohibited!” Informed of that, the Prophet, blessing and peace be upon him, said: “O people, it is not up to me to prohibit what God has made lawful to me, but is is a plant whose smell I detest.”

2 See the testimony of ‘Utbah b. Ghazwān in Muslim, *Ṣaḥīḥ*, vol. viii, p. 215, or Ibn Māja, *Sunan*, vol. ii, p. 1392, no 4156: “I saw myself the seventh of seven with the Messenger of God, blessing and peace be upon him. We did not have any food to eat except the leaves of plants, so that the corners of our mouths were ulcered.” See also, about the *ghazwat al-khabaṭ*, al-Ṭabarī, *Ta’rīkh*, trans. Fishbein, *Victory*, p. 149: “It was called the expedition of *al-khabaṭ* because they ate leaves beaten down from the trees (*khabaṭ*) until the linings of their mouths were like those of camels that have pastured on thorn trees.”

How would it not be so when many of the ulema – Ḥanafites and others – have issued *fatwā*s expounding its prohibition? It would consequently be necessary **[120]** to accuse them of error; now, to accuse of error many [scholars] is a difficult thing! In the Hijaz, some of the Mālikites have written the following answer to a question concerning the [tobacco] smoke:[1] "The use of [tobacco] smoke is prohibited just as is what it comes from (*aṣl*)." What it comes from is indeed some wood and fire, as it is constituted of particules of wood mixed with particules of fire. To use it is thus prohibited, as far as its fire particules are concerned, because the Most High has said: "Lo! Those who eat up, unjustly, the wealth of orphans, only eat up fire into their bellies."[2] This text proves the prohibitedness of fire. **[125]** The [tobacco] smoke originating from it is thus also prohibited.

Moreover, the Most High has made it one of the things by means of which [people] are tormented, as He said concerning the people of Jonah – peace be upon him: "When they believed, We drew off from them the torment of disgrace in this world's life."[3] The torment drawn off from them was smoke. In another verse He also said: "But watch you for the day when the sky will bring forth an evident smoke that will envelop humans. This will be a painful torment."[4] What is meant by the smoke mentioned in **[130]** this verse is what is really meant by the [word], according to what is said [by some scholars]; and, according to what these say, the noble [Qur'ānic] discourse says explicitly that smoke is a torment. Now, something by means of which a torment is inflicted, it is prohibited to use it. The jurists are agreed on the obliga-

1 Al-Laqānī (*Naṣīḥa*, Conclusion, p. 71), quoted here by al-Aqḥiṣārī, identifies this Mālikite as "our brother in God, Shaykh Khālid, professor at the Meccan Shrine, and shaykh of the Mālikites in the Hijaz" and quotes his letter in full. He is the Maghribī Khālid b. Aḥmad b. Muḥammad al-Ja'farī (d. 1043/1634); see al-Muḥibbī, *Khulāṣa*, vol. ii, p. 129. Al-Aqḥiṣārī's present quote of this letter ends l. 129, "...torment". He uses other passages of this letter, without indicating his source, in l. 131–134, l. 33–35, l. 44–46 (see pp. 35–36).

2 Qur'ān, *al-Nisā'* - 4:10.

3 Qur'ān, *Yūnus* - 10:98.

4 Qur'ān, *al-Dukhān* - 44:10–11.

tion to run away from a place of torment like Baṭn Muḥassir[1] – this term being an active participle derived from *al-taḥsīr*, "causing grief", and the name of a valley where God, Exalted is He, made the Companions of the Elephant perish.[2] If it is thus obligatory to run away from a place of torment, it shall *a fortiori* be obligatory to run away from something by means of which a torment gets inflicted.

[135] Furthermore, in those who use [tobacco] smoke, you see it coming out from their noses and their throats, [a condition] in which there is a resemblance to the people of the Fire and to those of the evil doers who will perish at the end of time; just as it is said in the *ḥadīth* that, at the end of time, there will be a smoke which will fill the earth, will dwell forty days over the humans and because of which the believer will be afflicted by a kind of catarrh; as for the infidel, it will come out from his two nostrils, his two ears[3] and his two eyes in such a way that the head of each of them will become like a roasted (*ḥanīdh*) head, i.e. a grilled one. Now, it is not proper for **[140]** the believer to resemble the people of the Torment, nor to use anything which is of the same kind as the Torment, nor anything which is part of the environment of the people of the Torment. A group of ulema[4] have detested the wearing of iron and copper rings because it is reported in the *ḥadīth* that they are the ornament of the people of the Fire.[5]

1 I.e. the valley of al-Muzdalifa; see Yāqūt, *Mu'jam*, vol. i, p. 533, no 1993.

2 Allusion to the failed expedition led with elephants against Mecca by the Yemenite king Abraha traditionally dated of around 570 C.E. and corresponding to the date of birth of the Prophet; see A. F. L. Beeston, *EI2*, art. *al-Fīl*. Some sources deny that Abraha's defeat took place in Baṭn Muḥassir; see the commentary of T. D. al-Nadwī in Mālik, *Muwaṭṭa'*, vol. ii, p. 397.

3 This tradition is not in the six canonic collections. In his *Tafsīr* (vol. xxvii, pp. 242–243), F. D. al-Rāzī quotes a version of it which he attributes to al-Zamakhsharī. The catarrh of the believers is mentioned in shorter versions of the tradition; see al Bukhārī, *Ṣaḥīḥ*, vol. vi, p. 114; Muslim, *Ṣaḥīḥ*, vol. viii, p. 130. See also al-Karmī, *Taḥqīq*, pp. 121–123.

4 Notably Ibn Taymiyya, explicitly referred to by al-Karmī (*Taḥqīq*, p. 124) in the passage here quoted by al-Aqḥiṣārī; see his *MF*, vol. iv, p. 16: "As for wearing earrings, bracelets, chains, fetters, as well as wearing iron and copper rings, it is an innovation […] it is wearing the outfits of the people of the Fire".

5 See notably Ibn Ḥanbal, *Musnad*, vol. ii, p. 179; al-Nasā'ī, *Sunan*, vol. viii, p. 172.

"A truthful brother told me that one of the great English merchants had procured him a snuffbox in which there was some tobacco and said to him: "This is the best kind of tobacco and the most perfect, because it is sprayed with pork fat after having been cooked with various kinds of drugs…"[1]

It is also true, according to what al-Bilālī[2] has mentioned in the *Epitome* of *The Revival* (*Iḥyā'*),[3] that [the Prophet], blessing and peace be upon him, used to detest hot food and to say: "God Most High did not feed us fire!"[4] This [tobacco] smoke is **[145]** even more to be detested because it is mixed with particules of fire, as already said. If,

1 I. al-Laqānī, *Naṣīḥa*, Section vii, p. 45. Drawing adapted from the frontispiece of E. R. Billings, *Tobacco*.

2 Muḥammad b. 'Alī al-Bilālī al-'Ajlūnī (d. 820/1417); see G. Brockelmann, *GAL*, *Suppl.*, vol. I, p. 749, no 10.

3 The *Iḥyā' 'ulūm al-dīn* of Abū Ḥāmid al-Ghazālī.

4 On this weak *ḥadīth* transmitted by Abū Hurayra, see al-Ghazālī, *Iḥyā'*, vol. ii, p. 367, trans. Zolondek, *Ādāb*, p. 31.

using it had no other [effect] than a blackening of the clothes and of the bodies, and the abomination of its smell and stink, it would be enough to hold back the intelligent individual from using it. Or, rather, if, by using it, one was doing nothing else than lending life to a custom of the infidels who have exported it and introduced it into the Islamic countries with the purpose* of harming the people of faith, it would be enough to urge the intelligent individual to avoid it, and to hinder him from engaging in it.

Note added in the margin of the MSS.* ***ADHKR**:*

Know that the first to have brought [tobacco smoking] to the country of the Rūm[1] are people from among the Nazarenes of the land called "England" (*Inklīz*). In his epistle which he titled *Advising the Brothers to Keep Away from Smoking* (*Naṣīḥat al-ikhwān bi-ijtināb al-dukhān*), Ibrāhīm al-Laqānī[2] said: "One of those who mix with the English Nazarenes has informed me that they only brought it to the countries of Islam because of this: they had taken a man who was among those smoking continuously and had died of burning of the liver, and had dissected him. They found that the smoke had penetrated his veins and nerves to such a point that the marrow of his bones had become black. They found his heart to be like a dry sponge with multiple and diverse holes in it, some of them big, others small, and they found that it was as if his liver had been grilled on fire. From that moment onwards, they forbade their people to continue using it and ordered it to be sold to the Muslims. They therefore exported it to the countries of Islam.

1 I.e. Ottoman Turkey, heir to the Roman Byzantine empire; see C. E. Bosworth, *EI2*, art. *Rūm*.

2 Abū l-Imdād Burhān al-Dīn Ibrāhīm b. Ibrāhīm al-Laqānī (d. 1041/1631), Mālikite professor at the Mosque of al-Azhar in Cairo, who also authored a *Jawharat al-tawḥīd*. His *Naṣīḥa* was completed in 1025/1616; see G. Brockelmann, *GAL*, vol. ii, pp. 412–413; *Suppl.*, vol. ii, pp. 436–437. It is edited by A. M. Āl Maḥmūd. He refers to English tobacco imports into Islamic countries in *Naṣīḥa*, Section vii, p. 38, 41, 45 (see the excerpt translated *supra*, p. 58); Section x, p. 53; Conclusion, p. 68 (the passage quoted here). He also mentions imports from the Maghreb and the Sudan, as well as local Muslim production. On the introduction of tobacco to

[150] The natures of most of the people of this time are however rigid, reluctant to comply, perpetually leaning towards that which should not concern them.[1] If some advice is given to them, they do not accept it but, rather, say: "[Smoking] has no place among the things about which we have been warned (*mu'tabarāt*), nor is the object of any opinion transmitted (*naql*) from the trustworthy Ancients!" They conceal the manifest reality and abstain from speaking the truth as, indeed, it had not yet appeared in the time of the trustworthy Ancients, so as to have its status made clear, among the things about which we have been warned. On the contrary, it only appeared at the beginning of the eleventh century and became an enormous calamity (*fitna*) for the whole of humanity as its consumption **[155]** spread, in [all] the countries, among men, women, and the young. It is thus obligatory on the ulema of this time to make clear its status to the people of faith.

It is not unlikely that such a development, in these days, is similar to the development that took place in earlier times, when hashish (*ḥashīsh*) appeared, which is made from the leaves of hemp (*qunnab*) and is called *al-banj*.[2] As its corruptive nature had not yet become apparent during the time of the independent legists (*mujtahid*) – the initiators of the four legal schools –, it remained considered as **[160]** fundamentally allowed like the rest of the plants, as explained by the imām al-Nasafī[3] in his *Fatwās*. "As soon as it appeared," he said, "in the time of al-Muzanī,[4]

Turkey by "English infidels" about 1009/1600–1010/1601, see also I. Peçevi, quoted in B. Lewis, *Istanbul*, p. 134; Kātib Çelebi, *Mīzān*, trans. Lewis, *Balance*, pp. 50–51.

1 Al-Karmī has similarly a very negative opinion of his contemporaries; see his *Taḥqīq*, p. 161.

2 On the various meanings of *banj*, see Y. Michot, *Opium*, p. 31, n. 1. Cannabis was eaten by Muslims for recreational purposes as early as the end of the 5th/11th century. On the use of cannabis in medieval Muslim society, see F. Rosenthal, *Herb*; Y. Michot, *Haschich*.

3 Ḥāfiẓ al-Dīn Abū l-Barakāt 'Alī b. Aḥmad al-Nasafī (d. 710/1310), important Ḥanafite jurisconsult and theologian, disciple of al-Kardarī; see W. Heffening, *EI2*, art. *al-Nasafī*, iv; A. Özel, *Alimleri*, pp. 74–75.

4 Abū Ibrāhīm Ismā'īl b. Yaḥyā al-Muzanī (Egypt, 175/791–264/878), disciple of al-Shāfi'ī and champion of his school of jurisprudence; see W. Heffening, *EI2*, art. *al-Muzanī*.

the companion of the imām al-Shāfi'ī, and its [use] reached alarming proportions, al-Muzanī issued a fatwā expounding its prohibition." Moreover, when [hashish] moved along towards the countries of 'Irāq, Abū Ḥafṣ al-Kabīr,[1] the disciple of Muḥammad b. al-Ḥasan,[2] the companion of Abū Ḥanīfa, was asked for a fatwā about it, before its corruptive nature had become apparent in 'Irāq. At first, he answered that it was lawful, on the basis of the fundamental allowedness [of things]. Thereupon, when its corruptive nature became clear, he revoked **[165]** the fatwā which he had first issued and issued a fatwā expounding its prohibition, similarly to the fatwā that al-Muzanī had issued. So, now, the fatwās of the people of the two legal schools – I mean the Shāfi'ite and the Ḥanafite – declare it prohibited.

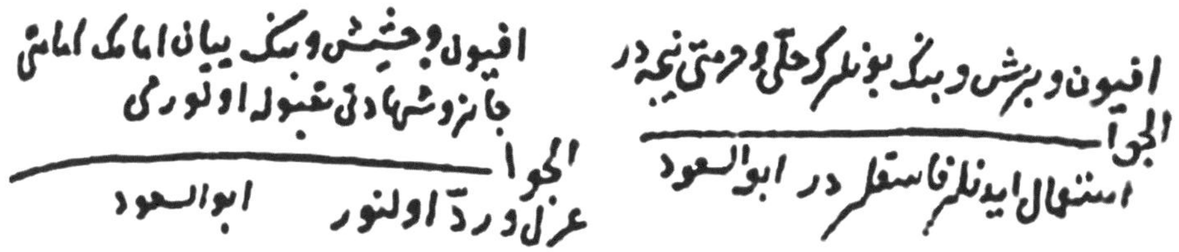

Two Ebüssuūd fatwās on banj *and other drugs*[3]

In his *Manẓūma*, al-'Alā'ī[4] counts eating [*banj*] among the great sins. In *al-Jāmi' al-saghīr* of al-Timirtāshī,[1] it is mentioned that the Sun of

1 Abū Ḥafṣ al-Kabīr, Aḥmad b. Ḥafṣ (d. 216/831), Ḥanafite jurisconsult; see A. Özel, *Alimleri*, p. 20. "A mufti of Bukhārā, and a very rigid Musalmān. He was surnamed Al-Kabīr, the Great, to distinguish him from his son [...] also a learned teacher" (H. G. Keene, *Dictionary*, p. 19).

2 Muḥammad b. al-Ḥasan b. Farqad al-Shaybānī, Abū 'Abd Allāh (d. in Khurāsān, 189/805?), important Ḥanafite jurist; see É. Chaumont, *EI2*, art. *al-Shaybānī*; see A. Özel, *Alimleri*, pp. 16–18.

3 Marginal notes of MS. **R**, f. 55v. Left: "For an imām eating opium, *hashīsh* and *banj*, is it [still] permitted to be an imām? And can his testimony be accepted? Answer: He shall be dismissed, and it shall be rejected (Abū l-Su'ūd)." Right: "To what degree are opium, bersh and *banj* lawful and prohibited? Answer: Those who use them are perverts (Abū l-Su'ūd)." For other fatwās of Ebüssuūd (d. 982/1574) on drugs, see M. E. Düzdağ, *Hayatı*, pp. 229–230, nos 694–702.

4 This author is identified in a marginal note of MS. **R**, f. 55v: "'Alā' al-Dīn al-Turkistānī in his *Manẓūma*, in which he expounded the number of great sins". He is 'Alā' al-Dīn b. al-Turkmānī, Abū l-Ḥasan 'Alī b. 'Uthmān (d. 750/1349), a

the imāms, al-Kardarī,[2] was asked about its lawfulness and its prohibitedness. "Nothing is reported from Abū Ḥanīfa and his companions concerning its lawfulness and its prohibitedness," he said, "because, in their time, eating it had not yet become a public phenomenon (*ẓahara*). Rather, it **[170]** was still done under cover (*mastūr*), and retained its status of being fundamentally allowed, as is the case with the rest of the plants, until the time of the imām al-Muzanī, the disciple of the imām al-Shāfiʿī. As, in his time, eating it openly had gained ground, as its consumption had spread and as the people's desire to eat it had become overwhelming, the imām al-Muzanī issued a fatwā expounding its prohibition. The corruptive nature of [*banj*] became first apparent in Arab ʿIrāq, whilst the imām al-Muzanī was in Baghdād. His fatwā was brought to Asad b. ʿAmr,[3] the disciple of Abū Ḥanīfa, who said that it was allowed. But when the calamity of its [use] became general and the fascination (*fitna*) that it exerted spread everywhere, when **[175]** the propagation of its evils became as effective as it did and the propagation of its harms became apparent as it did, to a point where foolishness overcame the sages and stupidity overwhelmed the intelligent people, the imāms of Transoxiana all chose the view expressed by al-Muzanī in his fatwā that eating it was prohibited and they agreed upon its prohibition."[4]

Ḥanafite chief qāḍī of Egypt, polygraph and author of a *Manẓūma fī l-kabāʾir*; see S. Polat, *İA*, art. *İbnü't-Türkmānī, Alāeddin*; A. Özel, *Alimleri*, p. 82.

1 Abū Ṣāliḥ Shams al-Dīn Muḥammad b. ʿAlī b. Shihāb al-Dīn al-Timirtāshī al-Ghazzī (d. 1004/1595), author of an important treatise of Ḥanafite applied *fiqh*, *Tanwīr al-abṣār wa jāmiʿ al-biḥār*; see C. Brockelmann, *GAL*, vol. ii, p. 404, no 6; *Suppl.*, vol. ii, p. 429, no 6; A. Özel, *Alimleri*, p. 133.

2 Al-Kardarī, Shams al-Aʾimma Abū l-Wajd Muḥammad b. ʿAbd al-Sattār b. Muḥammad al-ʿImādī (d. 642/1244), Ḥanafite jurist; see G. Brockelmann, *GAL*, *Suppl.*, vol. i, pp. 653–654; A. Özel, *Alimleri*, pp. 65–66.

3 Abū l-Munẓir Asad b. ʿAmr (d. 190/806), student of Abū Ḥanīfa and qāḍī of Baghdād and Wāsiṭ; see O. Çeker, *İA*, art. *Esed b. Amr*; A. Özel, *Alimleri*, p. 18.

4 This answer of al-Kardarī corresponds to, and in some way complements, the text sketching the history of hashish in Islam which F. Rosenthal found in the MS. *Gotha 1451* (= Pertsch, No 2096), f. 6a–b, and translated in his *Herb*, pp. 48–49. For Rosenthal, the idea that "hashish was commonly used in the Muslim east since the ninth century and already about this time was dealt with as a great danger to

In his *Commentary* (*Sharḥ*) on al-Qudūrī,[1] al-Ḥaddādī[2] has said: "The prohibition of [*banj*] is however less [severe] than the prohibition of wine. For somebody eating it, there is no Legal sanction (*ḥadd*), even if he gets drunk therefrom, but it is obligatory to punish him (*ta'zīr*). It is like drinking **[180]** urine and eating faeces: it is prohibited, there is no Legal sanction (*ḥadd*) for it, but it is obligatory to punish it (*ta'zīr*)."[3]

Since the fatwās of the ulema, from previous times, have confirmed the prohibition of the *banj* that had been brought about after the time of the independent legists, for the reason that its corruptive nature had [then] become apparent, it necessarily follows that thereunder shall also fall all these things that have been invented after their time and whose corruptive nature is apparent, like smoking, about which we have already spoken.

society by both Shāfi'ites and Ḥanafites" is "pure fancy and dictated by professional self-interest, although for all we really know it just might have been true in substance" (*Herb*, p. 49).

"It is reported in some of the books of the shaykhs that the *banj* eater (*banjī*) and the opium addict are not fit to be among the righteous and among the people entitled to be witnesses; let alone, *a fortiori*, to be among the pious (*ahl al-taqwā*) and those enjoying [God's] Friendship (*wilāya*). People unable to fast the fasting of Ramaḍān, which is one of the pillars of Islam, how could they be among [God's] Friends (*walī*)?" (MS. **R**, f. 58v, marginal note).

1 Abū l-Ḥusayn Aḥmad b. Muḥammad Aḥmad b. Ja'far b. Ḥamdān al-Qudūrī l-Baghdādī (d. 428/1037), Ḥanafite jurist, author of a celebrated juristic compendium, *al-Mukhtaṣar*; see M. Ben Cheneb, *EI2*, art. *al-Ḳudūrī*; A. Özel, *Alimleri*, pp. 33–34.

2 Abū Bakr b. 'Alī b. Muḥammad al-Ḥaddād(ī) l-'Abbādī al-Yamanī; see *supra*, p. 45–46, n. 3. The text of al-Ḥaddādī's ruling preceding the passage quoted here by al-Aqḥiṣārī is given in a marginal note of MS. **R**, f. 55v: "It is not permitted to eat the *banj* and the *hashish* which are made from the leaves of hemp (*qunnab*), nor opium (*afyūn*). This is all prohibited because it corrupts the reason, the complexion, causes other [types] of corruption and turns away from the remembrance of God Most High, from praying and from other actions of [religious] obedience. The prohibition of this is however… (From *The Shining Lamp* of al-Ḥaddādī)".

3 On this ruling of al-Ḥaddādī, see F. Rosenthal, *Herb*, p. 126.

"One coffee-house was opened after another, and men would gather together, with great eagerness and enthusiasm, to drink. Drug-addicts in particular, finding it a life-giving thing, which increased their pleasure, were willing to die for a cup..."[1]

Likewise, also, for coffee, this new invention which exerts a general fascination and whose calamitous [vogue] is so widespread[2] that it has become the cause **[185]** of various sorts of acts of disobedience and various types of forbidden behaviour. Using it necessarily forces one to observe these forbidden behaviours during gatherings, to mingle with the fools and the vile, to receive it from the hands of beardless youths,[3]

1 Kātib Çelebi, *Mīzān*, trans. Lewis, *Balance*, p. 60. Engraving from A. I. Melling, *Voyage*, pl. 26.

2 Coffee spread to the Ottoman capital around 957/1550; see R. S. Hattox, *Coffee*; Y. Michot, *Opium*, pp. 34–50.

3 Just as beautiful boys were employed in public baths to attract customers and care for their various needs, their rôle in coffee-houses was often sexually ambiguous,

to touch their hands, and to commit acts of disobedience. Now, all this violates manliness (*murū'a*) and brings down probity (*'adāla*). "It is not permitted to anybody," the legists have said, "to contribute to the tarnishing of his probity by committing actions demonstrating his vileness." "Every thing," they also said, "which is the cause of an act of disobedience is prohibited, and every **[190]** thing whose corruptive nature is known to be like the corruptive nature of things with which a [divine] threat is associated, or a Legal sanction, or a curse, is a great sin." Now, how little coffee is free from any of these [aspects]! It is thus incumbent upon the intelligent person to keep away from it, totally; all the more so as, by continuing to drink it, some harm is produced which affects the body when one abstains from it. Many of the ulema have issued fatwās prohibiting it, among whom the *muftī* of the Rūm, pre-eminent in all the sciences, the late Abū l-Su'ūd.[1] "What do you say about the coffee which the Muslims **[195]** drink in most countries, specially in the two Noble Sanctuaries? Is it allowed or not? Give us a fatwā, and you will be rewarded by God, the Most High!" When he was asked this question about [coffee, Abū l-Su'ūd] answered by saying: "To issue a fatwā allowing something which the adepts of debauchery apply themselves eagerly to engage in is among the things that anybody afraid of God Most High and fearing Him would hardly ever undertake!"

when coffee was served from their hands; see R. S. Hattox, *Coffee*, pp. 109–110; W. G. Andrews & M. Kalpaklı, *Age*, pp. 283–288.

1 The famous Sheykhülislām Meḥmed Abū l-Su'ūd Efendi (Ebüssuūd). This fatwā does not correspond to any of the three Abū l-Su'ūd fatwās on coffee published in M. E. Düzdağ, *Hayatı*, pp. 235–236, nos 722–724. The praise of Abū l-Su'ūd by somebody as close to Birgivī as al-Aqḥiṣārī may seem strange as Birgivī is usually considered as having been the arch-rival of the great muftī (see Kātib Çelebi, *Mīzān*, trans. Lewis, *Balance*, pp. 128–131). However, whatever the controversies that opposed them to each other, one should not forget that Birgivī and Abū l-Su'ūd were sometimes united in their opposition to Sufism; see. A. Y. Ocak, *Oppositions*, pp. 610–611.

Central Asian opium eaters[1]

Likewise, moreover, for opium (*afyūn*), bersh (*barsh*) and the rest of the corruptive substances (*mufsidāt*).[2] Someone consuming them in a quantity which does not **[200]** muddle his reason and his senses, nor is noxious to his body, is permitted to do so as it is devoid of what would necessarily entail a sin, no matter whether it is some necessity (*ḍarūra*) which induces him to consume them, or not. It is however incumbent upon the intelligent person not to take them except because of a need, after knowing his [own] temperament (*mizāj*) if he is knowledgeable about the temperaments, or after being informed by a skilful physician, expert in the temperaments, that such and such quantity of such and such corruptive substance does not affect such and such temperament in such and such season. If some doubt arises, it is compulsory for him to keep away from it. If he dares **[205]** to consume it, he is sinning, even if he remains safe and sound, and he shall ask God Most High to forgive

1 Drawing by Sedoff, in B. Vereschaguine, *Voyage*, p. 217.

2 On opium addiction in Ottoman society and the religious controversies concerning it, see Y. Michot, *Opium*.

him for having taken that risk and not having cared about its prohibition.

"For someone who is afflicted by the [habit of] eating opium, similar sorts of bersh and the rest of corruptive [substances], and has reached a point where he is himself afraid of dying if he abstains from it," some of the later authors have said,[1] "it is permitted to use the quantity of it which will not affect his reason and his senses; he nevertheless must make every conceivable effort **[210]** to reduce it and, [finally], to stop taking it, just as he must turn to God in repentance and regret his past addiction to it. In his *Commentary* (*Sharḥ*) on al-Qudūrī, al-Ḥaddādī has indeed said: "Opium is prohibited."

"Expounding the status – lawful or prohibited – of every newly invented thing is not done but by means of an analogic syllogism (*qiyās*). Now, the door of the analogic syllogism is shut in this time.[2] [This door] is indeed particular to the independent legal thinker (*mujtahid*); the time of independent legal thinking (*ijtihād*) has become extinct and its people have passed away. So, in the *Khulāṣa*,[3] it is mentioned that one of the jurists said **[215]** to al-Ṣadr al-Shahīd:[4] "You are an independent legal thinker". Al-Ṣadr al-Shahīd then said to him: "O jurist! Independent legal thinking is gone with its people! Myself, if I know the sayings of the ulema and report them correctly, what [divine] grace could be greater than that?" In the [*Khulāṣa*], it is also mentioned that when, a

[1] In his treatise on the lawfulness of coffee, 'Abd al-Qādir al-Jazīrī (d. *c*. 977/1570) quotes a fatwā of the Yemeni Shāfi'ite qāḍī Aḥmad b. 'Umar al-Muzajjad (d. 930/1524) making it "compulsory" (*wājib*) for the opium addict to take some of it on a regular basis in order not to die; see the translation in Y. Michot, *Opium*, pp. 31–32, 80.

[2] A similar objection appears in 'Abd al-Nāfi', *Talkhīṣ*, pp. 179–180: "Where is the independent legal thinker? (*Fa-ayna l-mujtahid?*)". On the so-called "closure of the door of *ijtihād*" in the 5th/11th century, see W. B. Hallaq, *Gate*.

[3] Name of various treatises. The one referred to here is probably the *Khulāṣat al-fatāwā* of the Ḥanafite *mujtahid* Iftikhār al-Dīn Ṭāhir b. Aḥmad al-Bukhārī (d. 542/1147); see A. Özel, *Alimleri*, pp. 48–49.

[4] 'Umar b. 'Abd al-'Azīz b. Māza, Abū Muḥammad, known as al-Ṣadr al-Shahīd (d. 536/1141), Ḥanafite uṣūlist from Bukhārā; see C. Brockelmann, *GAL*, vol. i, pp. 461–462; *Suppl.*, vol. i, pp. 639–640; A. Özel, *Alimleri*, pp. 44–45.

qāḍī having analogically related a question to another and pronounced a judgement, it becomes apparent on the strength of an earlier authoritative source (*riwāyat*[an]) that what is right is different [from his ruling], the defendant, on the Day of Resurrection, will be able to sue both the qāḍī and the claimant. The qāḍī will indeed have sinned by his independent legal thinking as, **[220]** in our time, there is nobody belonging to the people of independent legal thinking (*ahl al-ijtihād*). The claimant will have sinned by having, [for example], taken the money [attributed to him by this wrong judgement]. This being so, how would it be valid to speak of the lawfulness, or absence of lawfulness, [of a thing] in this time?"

Before the qāḍī[1]

If that[2] is said, the answer will be that the affirmation that the age of independent legal thinking is gone is debatable. Independent legal thin-

1 Drawing by F. Fau, in *Contes*, p. 18.
2 I.e. the objection developed in the preceding paragraph.

king has indeed no connection with a [particular] age, as has been made clear in its place. For somebody speaking about the questions that have been mentioned, it is thus possible to lay claim to thinking independently, on the basis of the right to pursue independent legal thinking even if **[225]** some people forbid it.

Does one not see that the companions of Abū Ḥanīfa – there is no divergence of opinion [about this] – are thinking independently? In spite of this, they indeed emulate (*qallada*) Abū Ḥanīfa in many questions and think independently in some. Moreover, in some of them such as Abū Yūsuf,[1] Muḥammad [al-Shaybānī] and their like, independent legal thinking may occur with the faculty of diverging. It might also be about something about which it is not reported from him[2] that he had divergent [views], as [is the case with] Ẓahīr al-Dīn,[3] Qāḍī-Khān[4] and their peers. This is why they have not been considered independent schools (*madhhab*) as al-Shāfi'ī, Mālik **[230]** and their like had been considered, since, fundamentally, there is nobody emulating them. What is mentioned in the *Khulāṣa* – [i.e.] that there is nobody belonging to the people of independent legal thinking in our time – is consequently to be understood as refering to the absolutely independent legal thinker (*mujtahid muṭlaq*) or to the one who has the faculty of diverging in some [matters]. This is proven by his words "it becomes apparent on the strength of an earlier authoritative source that what is right is different [from his ruling]", in this sense that he has no other proof thereof than a deficient investigation (*istiqrā'*), which does not help.

Some of the ulema are of the opinion that it is not possible for any time to be devoid of an independent legal thinker. It is also likely that

1 Abū Yūsuf Ya'qūb b. Ibrāhīm al-Anṣārī (d. 182/798), disciple of Abū Ḥanīfa and one of the founders of his school; see J. Schacht, *EI2*, art. Abū Yūsuf Ya'ḳūb.

2 I.e. Abū Ḥanīfa.

3 Ẓahīr al-Dīn al-Ḥasan b. 'Alī b. 'Abd al-'Azīz al-Marghīnānī (6th/12th c.), Ḥanafite jurist, teacher of Qāḍī-Khān; see W. Heffening, *EI2*, art. *al-Marghīnānī*.

4 Fakhr al-Dīn al-Ḥasan b. Manṣūr Qāḍī-Khān (d. 592/1196), Ḥanafite jurist and *mujtahid* from Transoxiana, famous for his manual of *fiqh* entitled *al-Fatāwā*; see Th. W. Juynboll & Y. Linant de Bellefonds, *EI2*, art. *Ḳāḍī Khān*; A. Özel, *Alimleri*, pp. 55–56.

the words of al-Ṣadr al-Shahīd, in the **[235]** anecdote mentioned, were just humility on his part. How would it not be so as Qāḍī-Khān was amongst his disciples? Now, in his *Fatwās*, how many there are of his sayings that are independent legal forms of thinking!

And even if one admitted the extinction of independent legal thinking, what has been mentioned [of the prohibition of a newly invented thing like tobacco smoking] would be a deduction (*takhrīj*), not an analogic syllogism. When the people of independent legal thinking formulate a universal rule – the latter being either regularly deriving from its object and what it is about, or known from what they say –, to make clear one of its particular elements is a deduction, not an analogic syllogism. Now, **[240]** nobody has the right to say: "The people of deduction have also become extinct, as they belong to the fourth class (*ṭabaqa*) of [scholars] according to the classification of one of the eminent authorities in an epistle of his!" It will indeed be said to him: "This is a claim without proof! The overflowing (*fayyāḍ*) [God], the Real, has not barred the door of [His] overflow to His servants. He is the One Giving Success and the One Helping. What a perfect Master and what a perfect Helper! And there is no power **[245]** and no might save in God, the High, the Great!"

[1]

[1] Young smoker. Detail of a bowl, Turkey, 11th/17th c. (Brussels, Musée du Cinquantenaire).

AḤMAD AL-RŪMĪ AL-AQḤIṢĀRĪ

Risāleh Dukhāniyyeh

Arabic text

Following the usage in Arabic editions, the text reads from the right and thus starts on p. 82.

ونحوهما ، إذ لا تقليد لهم لأحد أصلاً . فعلى هذا يكون ما ذُكِرَ في **الخلاصة** ، من أنّ أحداً ليس من أهل الاجتهاد في زماننا ، محمولاً على المجتهد المطلق والقادر على المخالفة في البعض . يدلّ عليه قوله « فظهر روايةً أنّ الحقّ بخلافه » على أنّه لا دليلَ له عليه إلاّ الاستقراء الناقص وهو لا يفيد .

فإنّ بعض العلماء ذهبوا على عدم جواز خلو الزمان عن المجتهد . وما ذُكِرَ من الحكاية يحتمل أنْ يكون تواضعًا من الصَدْرِ الشَهِيْد . كيف لا وقَاضِيْخَان من تلامذته ؟ وكم في **فتاواه** من أقواله الاجتهادية !

ولو سُلِّمَ انقراض الاجتهاد فما ذُكِرَ يكون تخريجًا لا قياسًا . فإنّ أهل الاجتهاد إذا ذكروا قاعدةً كليةً ، سواءً كانت منتظمة من موضوعها أو محمولها ، أو عُرِفَتْ من كلامهم ، فبيان جزئي من جزئياتها يكون تخريجًا لا قياسًا . وليس لأحد أنْ يقول : « قد انقرض أهل التخريج أيضًا لكونهم في الطبقة الرابعة على ما رتّبها[1] بعضُ الفضلاء في رسالة له ! » إذ يقال له : « هذا دعوى بلا دليل ! فإنّ الفيّاض الحقّ لم يسدّ على عباده باب الإفاضة . وهو الموفّق والمُعِيْن ، نِعْمَ المولى و نِعْمَ النصير[2] ! ولا حولَ ولا قوةَ إلاّ باللّه العلي العظيم ! »

تمّ تمّ
تمّ

١. رتبها ADKR : تبها H

٢. النصير A : المعين DHKR

على تناوله أَثِمَ ، وإنْ سلم ، ويستغفر اللّه تعالى من الجراءة وعدم مبالاته بالحرمة .

ومن ثمّه قال بعض المتأخّرين : « يجوز لمَن ابتلى بأكل الأفيون ونحوه من البرش وسائر المفْسدات وصار بحيث يخاف على نفسه مِن ترْكه الموت أنْ يستعمل منه القدْر الّذي لا يؤثّر في عقله وحواسّه ويجب عليه أنْ يسعى جهده في تقليله وقطعه كما يجب عليه أنْ يتوب إلى اللّه ويندم على ما مضى من تعاطيه ، إذ قد قال الحَدّادي في **شرح القُدُوْرِي** : « الأفيون حرام ! »

فإنْ قيل : « بيان الحكم من الحلّ والحرمة في كلّ ما حدث لا يكون إلاّ بالقياس ، وباب القياس مسدود في هذا الزمان لأنّه مختصّ بالمجتهد وقد انقرض زمان الاجتهاد ومضى أهله ، على ما ذُكر في **الخلاصة** أنّ فقيهاً من الفقهاء قال للصَدْرِ الشَهِيْدِ : « أنت مجتهد ! » فقال له الصَدْرُ الشَهِيْدُ : « أيّها الفقيه ، ذهب الاجتهاد مع أهله ، وأنا ، إذا عرفتُ أقوال العلماء وحكيتها على وجهها ، فأيّ نعمة أعظم منها ؟ » وذكر فيها أيضاً أنّ القاضي ، إذا قاس مسئلةً على مسئلة وحكم وظهر روايةً أنّ الحقّ بخلافه ، فالخصومة للمدّعى عليه يومَ القيامة على القاضي وعلى المدّعي لأنّ القاضي أثم بالاجتهاد إذ ليس أحد من أهل الاجتهاد في زماننا ، والمدعي أثم بأخْذ المال . فإذا كان كذلك فكيف يصحّ القول بالجواز وعدم الجواز في هذا الزمان ؟

فالجواب أنّ القول بذهاب عصر الاجتهاد فيه كلام . فإنّ الاجتهاد لا تعلّقَ له بالعصر كما بيّن في موضعه . فيمكن أنْ يُدّعى الاجتهاد فيما ذُكر من المسائل لمَن تكلّم فيها بناءً على ما هو الحقّ مِن تحرّي الاجتهاد وإنْ منعه البعض . ألا يُرى أنّ أصحاب [١٩٩ ظ] أبي حَنِيْفَة مجتهدون بلا خلاف[1] ، ومع هذا يقلّدون أبا حَنِيْفَة في كثير من المسائل ويجتهدون في بعضها ؟ ثمّ إنّ الاجتهاد في بعضهم قد يكون مع القدرة على المخالفة كأبي يُوْسُف ومحمّد وأمثالهما ، وقد يكون فيما لا رواية عنه على خلافه كظَهِيْر الدِيْن وقَاضِيْخَان ونظائرهما . ولهذا لم يُعَدّوا مذاهبَ مستقلّةً كما عُدّ الشَافِعِي ومَالِك

١. خلاف ADKR : ف H

فلمّا تحقّق فتوى العلماء في الزمان السابق على حرمة البنج المُحْدَث بعد زمن [١٩٨ ظ] المجتهدين لظهور فساده لزم أنْ يدخل فيها كلّ ممّا حدث بعد زمانهم وظهر فساده كالدخان الّذي مضى الكلام فيه .

وكالقهوة المُحْدَثة الّتي عمّت فتنتها[١] وشاعت بليتها بحيث كانت سببًا لأنواع المعاصي وأصناف المناهي . فيلزم استعمالُها مشاهدةَ[٢] تلك المنهيات في المحافل والمخالطةَ بالسفهاء والأراذل وتناولَها من أيدي المُرْد[٣] وغمزَ أيديهم وارتكابَ العصيان . وكلّ ذلك يُخلّ بالمروة ويسقط العدالة . وقد قال الفقهاء : « لا يجوز لأحد أنْ يتسبّب في إسقاط عدالته بارتكاب أفعال تدلّ على خساسته » . وقالوا أيضًا : « كلّ شيء يكون سببًا لمعصية فهو حرام ، وكلّ شيء عُلِمَ أنّ مفسدته كمفسدة ما قرن به الوعيد أو الحدّ أو اللعن فهو كبيرة » . فالقهوة قلّما تخلو عن شيء من ذلك ! فيتعيّن على العاقل اجتنابها بالكلّية ، مع أنّها يحصل بالمداومة عليها ضرارةٌ تؤثّر في البدن عند تركها . وقد أفتى بحرمتها كثيرٌ من العلماء ، من جملتهم مفتي الروم الفائق في جميع العلوم أبو السُعُوْد المرحوم . فإنّه لمّا سُئل عنها بأن قيل له : « ما قولكم في القهوة الّتي يشربها المسلمون في أكثر البلدان ، خصوصًا في الحرمين الشريفين ؟ هل هي مباحة أم لا ؟ أفتونا ، تكونوا مأجورين عند اللّه تعالى ! » أجاب بقوله : « الإفتاء بإباحة ما أكبّ أهلُ الفجور على تعاطيه ممّا لا يكاد يجترئ عليه مَن يخشى اللّه تعالى ويتّقيه » .

وكالأفيون والبرش وسائر المفْسدات . فإنّ مَن يتناول منها القدْر الّذي لا يشوّش العقل والحواسّ ولا يؤذي في البدن ، وإنْ جاز تناوله عند خلوه عمّا يوْجب الإثم ، سواءً دَعَتْ إلى تناوله ضرورةٌ أو لا ، لكنْ ينبغي للعاقل أنْ لا يتعاطاه إلاّ عن حاجة بعد معرفة مزاجه إنْ كان عالمًا بالأمزجة أو بعد إخبار طبيب ماهر عارف بالأمزجة بأنّ المقدار الفلاني من المفْسد [١٩٩ و] الفلاني لا يؤثّر في المزاج الفلاني في الفصل الفلاني ، فإنْ حصل شكّ يجب اجتنابه . وإنْ أقدم

١. فتنتها ADKR : فتنها H
٢. استعمالُها مشاهدةَ H : من استعمالها مشاهدةُ DKR مَن استعملها مشاهدةُ A
٣. المرد H : المردان ADKR

ولا يبعد أنْ يكون هذه الواقعة في هذه الأيّام كالواقعة الكائنة في سالف الزمان عند ظهور الحشيش الّذي يصنع من ورق القُنّب ويقال له « البَنْج » . فإِنّه لمّا لم يظهر فسادُه في زمن المجتهدين من أصحاب المذاهب الأربعة بقي على أصل الإِباحة كسائر النباتات ، كما صرح به الإِمام النَسَفي في [١٩٨ و] **فتاواه** فقال إنّه أوّل ما ظهر في زمن المُزَني ، صاحب الإِمام الشَافِعي ، وتفاقم أمره ، أفتى المزني بحرمته . ثمّ لمّا انتقل إلى بلاد العراق أُستفتي عنه أبو حَفْص الكَبِيْر ، تلميذ محمّد بن الحَسَن ، صاحب أبي حَنِيْفَة ، قبل ظهور فساده في العراق . فأجاب أوّلاً بالحلّ بناءً على الإِباحة الأصلية ، ثم لمّا تبيّن فساده رجع عمّا أفتى به أوّلاً وأفتى بحرمته كما أفتى بها المزني . والآن فتوى أهل المذهبين ، أعني الشافعي والحنفي ، على حرمته .

والعَلائِي في **منظومته** عدّ أكله من الكبائر . وذكر في **الجامع الصغير** للتِمرْتَاشِي أنّ شمس الأئمة الكَرْدَرِي سُئل عن حلّه وحرمته فقال : « لم يُنقل عن أبي حنيفة وأصحابه في حلّه وحرمته شيءٌ لأنّ أكله لم يظهر في زمانهم بل كان مستوراً ، باقيًا على الإِباحة الأصلية كما في سائر النباتات إلى زمن الإِمام المزني ، تلميذ الإِمام الشافعي . فإِنّه في زمانه لمّا فشى أكله وشاع تناوله وغلب[١] رغبة الناس في أكله أفتى الإِمام المزني بحرمته . وكان فساده أوّل ظهوره في عراق العرب والإِمام المزني في بغداد . وبلغ فتواه إلى أَسَد بن عَمْرو ، تلميذ أبي حنيفة ، فقال إنّه مباح . فلمّا عمّت بليته وشاعت فتنته ووقع ما وقع من انتشار شره وظهر ما ظهر من انتشار ضرره ، حتّى غلبت السفاهة على الحكماء وبهرت البلادة على العقلاء ، اِختار أئمّة ما وراء النهر بأسرهم ما أفتى به الإِمام المزني من حرمة أكله واتّفقوا على تحريمه » .

قال الحَدّادي في **شرح القُدُوْري** : « لكنّ تحريمه دون تحريم الخمر » . فإِنّ مَن أكله لا حدّ عليه ، وإن سكر منه ، بل يجب عليه التعزير ، كما إذا شرب البول وأكل الغائط فإِنّه حرام ولا حدّ عليه بل يجب عليه التعزير .

---

١. غلب ADKR : في + H

وعينيه حتّى يصير رأس أحدهم كالرأس الحنيذ ، أي المشوي ، فلا ينبغي للمؤمن أنْ يتشبّه بأهل العذاب ولا أنْ يستعمل ما هو من نوع العذاب ولا ما هو من ملابسات أهل العذاب ، وقد كره جمع من العلماء التختّم بالحديد والنُحاس لما جاء في الحديث إنّهما حلية أهل النار .

وصحّ على ما ذكره البِلاَلي في **مختصر الإحياء** أنّه عليه الصلاة والسلام كان يكره الطعام السخن ويقول : « إنّ اللّه تعالى لَم[1] يطعمْنا ناراً » . فهذا الدخان أوْلى بالكراهة لأنّه مختلط بأجزاء نارية كما مرّ . فلو لم يكن في استعماله إلاّ تسويد الثياب والأبدان وكراهة الريح والإنتان لكفى زاجراً للعاقل عن استعماله ، بل لو لم يكن في استعماله إلاّ إحياء سنّة الكفّار الّذين أخرجوه وأظهروه في بلاد الإسلام توصّلاً[2] إلى إضرار أهل الإيمان لكفى باعثاً للعاقل على اجتنابه ومانعاً عن ارتكابه .

لكنّ أكثر أهل الزمان طبائعهم جامدة صعبة الإنقياد مائلة دائماً إلى ما لا يعنيهم . إنْ نُصحوا لا يقبلون النصيحة بل يقولون : « ليس له محلّ في المعتبرات ولا نقل عن السلف الثقات ! » ويسترون الحقّ الصريح ويتركون القول الصحيح لأنّه لم يظهر في زمن السلف الثقات حتّى يبيّن حكمه في المعتبرات ، بل إنّما ظهر في أوائل القرن الحادي عشر وصار فتنةً عظيمةً على عامّة البشر إذ[3] شاع تناولُه في البلدان بين الرجال والنساء والصبيان . فلزم على علماء الزمان بيان حكمه لأهل الإيمان .

---

١. لم + ADKR : تعالى H

٢. أعلم أنّ أوّل مَن جلبه إلى برّ الروم قوم من نصارى الأرض الّتي يقال لها « إنكليز » . وقال إبراهيم اللقاني في رسالته الّتي سمّاها « **نصيحة الإخوان باجتناب الدخان** » : « قد أخبرني بعضُ المخالطين لنصارى الإنكليز أنّهم إنّما جلبوه إلى بلاد الإسلام لأنّهم أخذوا رجلاً ممّن كان يداوم عليه ومات باحتراق الكبد وشرّحوه فوجدو الدخان قد سرى في عروقه وعصبه حتّى أنّ مخّ عظامه قد اِسْوَدّ ، ووجدوا قلبه مثل السفنجة اليابسة ، وفيه أثقاب كثيرة متنوّعة ، بعضها كبير وبعضها صغير ، ووجدوا كبده كأنّه شوى على النار ، فمن ذلك الوقت منعوا قومهم من المداومة عليه وأمروا ببيعه للمسلمين وبهذا السبب أخرجوه إلى بلاد الإسلام » + $A^{m}D^{m}H^{m}R^{m}K^{m}$: توصلا

٣. إذ ADHR : إذا K

للفقراء الغذاء والإدام كما في غزوة خيبر الّتي كان فيها الثوم والكرّاث غالب ما يقتاتون حتّى قَرِحت أشداقهم . وليس هذا الدخان كذلك لأنّه لا يصلح لشيء من ذلك أصلاً ، فيكون القياس فاسداً لكونه قياساً بلا جامع .

كيف لا وقد أفتى بحرمته كثيرٌ من العلماء الحنفية وغيرهم ؟ فيلزم تخطئتهم وتخطئة كثير أمر عسير ! وقد كتب بعض المالكية في الديار الحجازية جوابًا عن سؤال يتعلّق بالدخان وهو أنّ استعمال الدخان حرام كأصله لأنّ أصله الخشب والنار لكونه أجزاءً من الخشب ممزوجةً بأجزاء من النار . فهو من حيث أجزائه النارية الّتي فيه يحرم استعماله لقوله تعالى : «إِنّ الّذِينَ يَأْكُلُونَ أَمْوَالَ الْيَتَامَى ظُلْمًا إِنّمَا يَأْكُلُونَ فِي بُطُونِهِمْ نَارًا» . فدلّ النصّ على حرمة النار ، فيحرم الدخان الحاصل منها .

وأيضًا إنّه تعالى جعله ممّا يعذّب به حيث قال في[١] حقّ قوم يونس عليه السلام : «لَمّا آمَنُوا كَشَفْنَا عَنْهُمْ عَذَابَ الْخزْيِ فِي الْحَيَاةِ الدُّنْيَا» . فإن العذاب المكشوف عنهم كان دخانًا . وقال في آية أخرى : «فَارْتَقِبْ يَوْمَ تَأْتِي السّمَاءُ بِدُخَانٍ مُبِينٍ ، يَغْشَى النّاسَ هَذَا عَذَابٌ أَلِيمٌ» . فإنّ المراد بالدخان المذكور في هذه الآية معناه الحقيقي على قول ، وعلى هذا القول يكون النظم الكريم صريحًا في كون الدخان[٢] عذابًا ، وما به التعذيب يحرم استعماله . فإنّ الفقهاء قد اتّفقوا على وجوب الفرار من محلّ العذاب كبَطْن مُحَسّر ، فإنه على لفظ إسم الفاعل من التحسير ، إسم وادٍ أهلك[٣] اللّه تعالى فيه أصحاب الفيل . فإذا وجب الفرار من محلّ العذاب فوجوب[٤] الفرار ممّا به العذاب أوْلى .

ثمّ إنّ المستعملين له تراهم أنّه يخرج من أنوفهم وحلوقهم وفيه تشبّه بأهل النار وبالّذين يهلكون في آخر الزمان من الأشرار كما جاء في الحديث أنّه يكون في آخر الزمان دخان يملأ الأرض يقيم على الناس أربعين يومًا ، أمّا المؤمن فيصيبه منه كهيئة الزكام [١٩٧ ظ] ، وأمّا الكافر فيخرج من منخريه وأذنيه

١. في + ADKR : قال H
٢. الدخان + ADKR : كون H
٣. واد أهلك ADKR : واذا هلك H
٤. فوجوب ADKR : فوجب H

عليهم وتزيينه لهم حتّى يتولّد من تكاثفه في عاقبة أمره إلا دواء . فإنّ تكراره يسوّد ما يقابله فيتولّد منه الحرارة فيكون في عاقبة أمره داءً لا دواءً . ثمّ يلزم على دعواهم أنْ يكون الناس كلّهم مرضى وأنْ يكون مرضُهم في جميع الفصول الأربعة من نوع واحد [١٩٦ ظ] وأنْ يكون معالجتُهم فيها بشيء واحد على جهة واحدة ، وبطلانه غير خفي على أحد من العقلاء .

ثمّ فيه إضاعة المال لأنّه يُشترى بثمن غالٍ فيدخل في الإسراف المحرّم ، مع نتن ريحه وأذيته لشامّيه الّذين لا يستعملونه ! وقد جاء في الحديث : « كلّ مُؤْذٍ في النار » . وقال المِكْنَاسِي : « الرائحة المُنْتِنة تخرق الخياشيم وتصل إلى الدماغ وتؤذي الإنسان . ولذلك قال النبي عليه الصلاة والسلام : « مَن أكل من هذه الشجرة فلا يقربنّ مسجدنا يؤذينا بريحه » . والمراد من هذه الشجرة جنس ما له رائحة كريهة يتأذّى بها الإنسان ، بدليل تعليله عليه الصلاة والسلام . والمعنى أنّ مَن أكل شيئًا ممّا له رائحة كريهة يتأذّى بها الإنسان فلا يقربنّ مسجدنا لأنّه يؤذينا برائحته الكريهة . وقد ثبت في **صحيح** مسلم أنّه عليه الصلاة والسلام كان ، إذا وجد من رجل في المسجد ريح البصل أو الثوم ، أمر به فأُخرج إلى البقيع . ولهذا قال الفقهاء : « كلّ مَن وُجد فيه رائحة كريهة يتأذّى بها الإنسان يلزم إخراجه من المسجد ولو بجرّه من يده أو رجله دون لحيته وشعر رأسه » . فعلى هذا يلزم إخراج كثير من الأئمة والمؤذّنين من المسجد والجامع في هذا الزمان لوجود الرائحة الكريهة فيهم بسبب مداومتهم على استعمال الدخان الكريه الرائحة ، بل إنّهم قد يستعملونه في داخل المسجد والجامع فيكون الكراهة في حقّهم أشدّ وأكثر .

وقد نُقل عن بعض المفتونين به أنّه كان يقول : « هو حلال ، وإلاّ لحرم البصل والثوم والكرّاث ! » وهذا القول منه فاسد لأنّ النصّ الوارد فيها لا يدلّ إلاّ على منع آكلها من قربان المسجد فقط إذ يلزم أنْ يؤذي المسلمين بريحها عند قربان المسجد وحضور الجماعة . وأمّا مَن أكلها ولم يقرب المسجد فالنصّ عنه ساكت . وإنّما يثبت حلّ أكلها من غير قربان المسجد بتقرير النبي عليه الصلاة والسلام على أكلها . وإلاّ لمنع منه كما منع من قربان المسجد ، مع أنّ بينها وبين الدخان فرقًا وهو أنّها من مصلحات الطعام [١٩٧ و] وممّا يكون

جَميعا » . فإنّه تعالى ذكره في معرض الامتنان ولا يكون الامتنان إلا بالنافع المباح . فكأنّه تعالى قال : « هو الّذي خلق لأجلكم جميع ما في الأرض من المنافع لتنتفعوا بها » . وعلى هذا القول الثالث الصحيح يخرج حكم هذا الدخان أيضًا .

فإنّه لو [١٩٦ و] كان نافعًا لكان الأصل فيه الإباحة ، لكن قد ثبت بأخبار الحذّاق من الأطبّاء أنّ مطلق الدخان مضرّ ولو في الآجل ، فيكون الأصل فيه الحرمة . بل لو وقع الشكّ في أمره لغلب جانب الحرمة كما هو القاعدة الشرعية . فإنه عليه الصلاة والسلام قال : « الحلال بيّن والحرام بيّن وبينهما مشتبهات لا يعلمهنّ كثير من الناس . فمَن اتّقى الشبهات فقد استبرأ لدينه وعرضه ، ومَن وقع في الشبهات وقع في الحرام كالراعي يرعى حول الحمى يوشك أنْ يرتع فيه » .

واختلف العلماء في حكم هذه الشبهات ، فذهب بعضهم إلى حرمتها لأنّه عليه الصلاة والسلام قد أخبر في هذا الحديث بأنّ مَن ترك ما اشتبه عليه حكمُه ولم ينكشف له حقيقةُ أمره يكون دينُه سالمًا ممّا يفسده أو ينقصه ونفسه ناجيًا ممّا يعيبه ويلام[1] عليه ومَن لم يتركْه بل فعله يقع في الحرام . وهذا الدخان ممّا اشتبه حكمُه ولم ينكشف حقيقةُ أمره ، فمَن تركه ولم يستعملْه يكون دينه سالمًا من الفساد أو النقصان ونفسه ناجيًا من العيب واللوم بين الأنام ، ومَن لم يتركْه بل استعمله يكون واقعًا في الحرام .

وذهب بعضهم إلى كراهتها لما جاء في حديث آخر أنّه عليه الصلاة و السلام قال : « الأمور ثلاثة ، أمر تبيّن لك رشدُه فاتّبعْه و[2]أمر تبيّن لك غيّه فاجتنبْه وأمر أُختلف فيه فدَعْ ما يُريبك إلى ما لا يُريبك » . ولا شكّ أنّ أمر الدخان ممّا أراب وأوقع في الاضطراب ، وأقلّ مراتبه الكراهة .

ولا يُظنّ أنّه ينتهي إلى درجة الإباحة بتعلّل كثير ممّن يتعاطاه أنّه نافع ودواء لكلّ داء وأنّهم وجدوا في استعماله دواءً لأمراضهم ، لأنّ ذلك من تلبيس إبليس

---

١. يلام ADKR : يلايم H

٢. أمر . . . و ADKR : *hom.* — H

ضعفًا في البدن وثقلاً في الأعضاء وغشاوةً في البصر وإمساكًا في الهاضمة ، وذلك لأنّه كما قال الأطبّاء مجفّف مع نوع حرارة . فيفعل في ابتدائه ما ذكروه أوّلاً وفي انتهائه ما ذكروه آخرًا .

على أنّه لو تحقّق نفعُه فبعد النفع يُمنع من استعماله لأنّه حينئذ يكون دواءً ولا يجوز استعمال الدواء بعد زوال المرض لأنّه إذا لم يجد مرضًا يزيله [١٩٥ ظ] يأخذ من البدن فيؤدّي إلى الضرر ، وما يؤدّي إلى الضرر يُمنع من استعماله . ألا يُرى أن الخمر المحرّمة بالنصّ قد أخبر القرآنُ بنفعها ، كما قال اللّه : « يَسْأَلُونَكَ عَنْ الْخَمْرِ وَالْمَيْسِرِ قُلْ فِيهِمَا إِثْمٌ كَبِيرٌ وَمَنَافِعُ لِلنَّاسِ » ، لكنّ جانب النفع إذا قابله جانب الضرر يحمي جانب الضرر حتّى قال الفقهاء : « لو كان في شيء وجوه متعدّدة توجب الحلّ والجواز ووجه واحد يوجب الحرمة وعدم الجواز يرجّح جانب الحرمة احتياطًا » .

فإنْ قيل إنّ المستعملين له يدّعون أنّهم يجدون عقيب استعماله خفّةً في البدن ، فكيف يصحّ القول بعدم النفع فيه ؟ فالجواب على ما ذكره بعض المتناولين له لتجربة نفعه وضرره أنّ المستعملين له في حال استعماله يحصل لهم ألم شديد وعند فراغهم عنه ينجون من ذلك الألم ويحصل لهم راحة ، فيظنّ هؤلاء المساكين أنّ تلك الراحة حصلت من استعماله ولا يدرون أنّها إنّما حصلت من خلاصهم عن استعماله .

ثمّ إنّ لنا في معرفة حرمة الأشياء وإباحتها وجهًا حسنًا يرجع إلى الأصول وهو أنّ الحقّ في الأشياء قبل البعثة أن لا يكون فيها حكم ، وبعد البعثة اختلف العلماء فيها على ثلاثة أقوال . الأوّل أنّها متّصفة بالحرمة إلاّ ما دلّ دليل شرعي[1] على إباحته . والثاني أنّها متّصفة بالإباحة إلاّ ما دلّ دليل شرعي[2] على حرمته . والثالث ، وهو الصحيح ، أن يكون فيها تفصيل ، وهو أنّ المضارّ متّصفة بالحرمة بمعنى أنّ الأصل فيها الحرمة وأنّ المنافع متّصفة بالإباحة بمعنى أنّ الأصل فيها الإباحة لقوله تعالى : « هُوَ الَّذِي خَلَقَ لَكُمْ مَّا فِي الأَرْضِ

---

١. شرعي N : الشرعي H الشرع ADKR

٢. شرعي N : الشرعي H الشرع ADKR

في العبث ، بل هو بالعبث أنسبُ لخلوه عن اللذّة الّتي في اللعب واللهو . اللّهمّ إلاّ أن يستلذّه نفوسُ بعض المستعملين له بتسويل شيطاني ! فحينئذ يدخل في اللعب أو اللهو .

وعلى أيّ وجه كان فهو عارٍ عن الفائدة الدينية ، وهو ظاهر ، وعن الفائدة الدنيوية أيضًا لأنّه لا يصلح لشيء من الغذاء أو الدواء أصلاً ، بل هو مضرّ لاتّفاق الأطبّاء على أنّ مطلق الدخان مضرّ . قال ابن سينا : « لولا الدخان والقتام لعاش ابن آدم ألف عامّ » . وقال جالينوس : « اجتنبوا ثلاثة وعليكم بأربعة ولا حاجة لكم إلى الطبيب[١] . اجتنبوا الدخان والغبار والنتن [١٩٥ و] وعليكم بالدسم والحلو والطيب والحمام » . وذُكر في **القانون** أن جميع أصناف الدخان مجفّف بجوهره الأرضي وفيه نارية يسيرة . قال بعض الفضلاء : « فإذا كان جميع أصناف الدخان مجفّفًا يكون هذا الدخان مجفّفًا للرطوبات البدنية فيكون مؤدّيا إلى حصول أمراض كثيرة » . فلا يجوز استعماله لوجوب صيانة النفس عن لحوق الضرر ، وقد ذُكر في **نصاب الاحتساب** أنّ استعمال المضرّ حرام .

فإنْ قيل : « بعض الأطبّاء قد يعالجون بعض الأمراض ببعض أصناف الدخان ويشاهَد نفعُه . فكيف يصحّ المنعُ عن استعمال جميع أصنافه ؟ » فالجواب أنّهم إنّما يعالجون به لحظةً يسيرةً ، لا على الدوام ، حتّى يحصل ما ذُكر من التجفيف .

فإنْ قيل : « ما ذُكر من التجفيف لا يضرُ في البَلْغَمي لكثرة رطوباته وانتفاعه بتجفيفها . فما وجه المنع عن هذا الدخان ؟ » فالجواب أنّ حدّ الانتفاع به مجهول . فلا بدّ في معرفة ذلك من طبيب حاذق عارف بالأمزجة والقدْر الّذي يُنتفع به . وإلاّ فالإقدام عليه حرام مطلقًا لوقوع التردّد بين السلامة وعدمها . فإنّ العدول من مستعمليه قد اختلفوا فيه ، فمنهم مَن يقول بضرره ومنهم مَن يقول بعدم ضرره ومنهم مَن يشكّ فيه . لكنّ الفريق الأغْلب الّذي جانبُ الحقّ إليه أقْربُ يقول إنّه يُحْدث في ابتدائه قوّةً في الجسم وحدّةً في البصر ونشاطًا في الأعضاء وهضمًا في الطعام . فإذا حصلت المداومة يُوْرث

١. الطبيب ADK^{m}R : الطيب HK

الرسالة الدخانية

للشيخ أحمد الرومي الاقحصاري

بسم الله الرحمن الرحيم

الحمد للّه والصلاة والسلام على رسول اللّه وعلى آل رسول اللّه .

وبعد ، فقد ظهر في هذا الزمان من قبل الكفرة العدوة لأهل الإيمان ورقُ نبتٍ يقال له « الدخان » وأُبْتُلِيَ بشرب دخانه كافّةُ الأنام من الخواصّ والعوامّ . فوجب على علماء الدين بيانُ حكمه للمسلمين : هل يحلّ استعمالُه أم يجب اجتنابُه ؟ فاستمعوا يا أولي الألباب ما يقال لكم في هذا الباب قد كثر فيه الأقاويل !

والحقّ الّذي عليه التعويل أنّ الفعل الاختياري الصادر عن المكلّف ، إن لم يترتّب عليه فائدةٌ دينية أو دنيوية ، فهو دائر بين العبث واللعب واللهو . وفي كتب اللغة لم يفرّقْ بين هذه الثلاثة لكنّ لا بدّ من الفرق لعطف بعضها على بعض في القرآن . وهو ، على ما ذكره بعض الفحول وكان حقيقًا بالقبول ، أنّ العبث الفعل الّذي ليس فيه لذّة ولا فائدة . وأمّا الّذي فيه لذّة بلا فائدة فهو لعب ، ومثله اللهو إلاّ أنّ فيه زيادة حظّ النفس بحيث تشتغل بها عمّا يهمّها . والكلّ حرام لأنّها لم تُذْكَرْ في القرآن إلا على طريق الذمّ . فلما عُلم حرمة هذه الثلاثة عُلم حرمة استعمال هذا الدخان لدخوله إمّا في اللعب أو في اللهو أو

Appendix

Sinān al-Dīn al-Amāsī on Opium and Coffee

IN *Opium*, pp. 113–108 and 97–107, I have edited and translated into French a short anonymous Arabic text prohibiting opium and praising coffee, on the basis of two pages added, after the *Majālis al-abrār* of Aḥmad al-Rūmī al-Aqḥiṣārī, in MS. *Michot 0402*, ff. 285v–286r (**M**; see the photos, plates I-II). I am now able to identify the origin of that text: the *Tabyīn al-maḥārim – The Exposition of Prohibited Things* of the Ḥanafite Khalwatī shaykh Yūsuf Sinān al-Dīn al-Amāsī (d. 986/1578),[1] *Chapter on wine and gambling*.

This being known, two mistakes for which I ask the indulgence of the scholars must be corrected.

The first two of the last four words of my edition of the **M** text on opium and coffee (*Opium*, p. 108, ll. 5: *tabayyana l-maḥārim…*, plate II) are not part of this text itself but indicate from which source it is borrowed and should read *Tabyīn* (not *Tabayyun*) *al-maḥārim…* Accordingly, the end of the translation (p. 106–107) must become: « En somme, n'iront l'interdire qu'un ignorant ou un fanatique (*muta'aṣṣib*). ([Tiré] de *L'exposé des choses interdites…*) »[2]

In *Opium*, p. 63–64, it was wrong to think that the person who added the text on opium and coffee to **M** might have been its original author. The external evidence for dating this addition to around 1100/1700 is not affected by this correction. As for the original source of the text

1 On al-Amāsī, see Kh. D. al-Ziriklī, *A'lām*, vol. viii, p. 233; C. Brockelmann, *GAL*, vol. ii, p. 507; *Suppl.*, vol. ii, pp. 452, 525. His death is also dated to 936/1530 (*www.yazmalar.gov.tr*) and 1000/1591 (*GAL*).

2 As for the last two words of my edition of the **M** text on opium and coffee (*Opium*, p. 108, ll. 6: *min 'ayni-hi*, plate II), they are also not part of this text itself but I am not sure anymore how to read them. They are perhaps an ending logographic formula (*minhiyya*) asking for God's mercy: *min-hu – raḥima-hu Allāh*, "From him – may God be merciful to him" (see A. Gacek, *Supplement*, p. 74).

quoted, it must obviously be dated to the lifetime of al-Amāsī, i.e. the 10th/16th century.

Here is a translation of the pages of al-Amāsī's *Tabyīn* corresponding to the text on opium and coffee in **M**.[1] As already noted in relation to the latter text,[2] the positions they express about opium and coffee come in sharp contrast with the views of al-Aqḥiṣārī.

"Section on eating *banj*, which is a prohibited herb (*ḥashīsh*). As for opium, it is prohibited according to Muḥammad [al-Shaybānī], in small and large [quantities]. In the *Shining Lamp*, [al-Ḥaddādī] said: "Opium is prohibited", without binding its prohibition to the sayings of anyone. This [prohibition] is indeed manifest, as it is harmful to the body and [the scholars] have said that it is prohibited to eat any of the things that are harmful to the body.

Moreover, it spoils the morality [of a person], weakens the intelligence and the body, and does not enable to fulfill many of the obligations [of the religion]. One thus sees many of those for whom eating opium is an habit not being able to fast Ramaḍān, as is observed in our time. Also, an [opium eater] makes many mistakes in his prayer: he does not know how many *rak'a*s to pray and he pays little attention to what his imām does.[3] The opium addict is indeed continuously drowsy, apart from only a few moments.

Somebody told me [the following story]. One night, he said, we were praying the last prayer of the evening (*'ishā'*), and one of the opium eaters was praying with us. When he prostrated with us for the first prostration of the [first] *rak'a*, he [fell asleep]. We rose up from this prostration whereas he remained prostrated and didn't rise up. We

1 I read these pages of the *Tabyīn* in MS. Ankara, Milli Kütüphane, *Nevşehir Damad İbrahim Paşa İl Halk Kütüphanesi*, 50 Damad 253, ff. 31r–32r (dated 980/1572). The differences from the text on opium and coffee in **M** are minimal and not reported. They become clear when this English version is compared with its translation in Y. Michot, *Opium*, pp. 98–107. When authors and works mentioned in these pages of the *Tabyīn* have already been identified *supra*, no footnote will be added here.

2 See *supra*, pp. 28–29.

3 Literaly, "to the state (*ḥāl*) of his imām".

prayed [the rest of] the prayer, concluded it, and went back to our homes while he stayed prostrated, in the same state. When the morning rose, we came to the mosque and found him prostrated as we had left him! He had stayed prostrated, in the same prostration of the last prayer of the evening, until the morning!

"We rose up from this prostration whereas he remained prostrated and didn't rise up..."[1]

[1] Turkish miniature (2d half of the 17th c.); see F. Taeschner, *Volksleben*, pl. 30.

When something plunges [one] into such a state, there is no doubt that it is prohibited. The drunkard is indeed withheld from praying because he does not know how to pray, nor how to recite [the *sūra*s in the prayer]. Which is why wine has been prohibited. It is indeed the reason why one turns away from praying and remembering God Most High!

Opium similarly turns one away from praying and fasting because, most of the time, the opium addict does not know how to pray, nor how many prayers to do. How often he stays there, standing, without reciting [any *sūra*], as he is so drowsy! And when he sits down to bear witness [that there is no god but God and that Muḥammad is the Messenger of God], he perhaps forgets to recite the salutations [to be addressed to God]. How often, also, [at the end of the prayer], he omits saying "Peace be upon you!" and comes out of his prayer without having said it. For us, [the Ḥanafites, to say "Peace be upon you!" at the end of the prayer] is however obligatory (*wājib*), and his prayer is thus defective. For al-Shāfi'ī, it is an injunction (*farḍ*), and his prayer is thus null.

To sum up, most of the time the opium addict is not able to do the prayer the way he is commanded to do it, just as most of them are unable to fast Ramaḍān, as observed. If the vice (*fasād*) of opium had spread in the time of Abū Ḥanīfa – may God have mercy on him – as it has spread in our time, he would have issued a fatwā prohibiting it without ambiguity (*shubha*). Do you not see that when *banj* appeared, al-Muzanī issued a fatwā prohibiting it, whereas the other [scholars] opposed him? When however appeared, of this vice, what appeared of it, they all issued fatwās prohibiting it.

Every thing which, when it is eaten or drunk, withholds one from fulfilling one of the injunctions [of the religion] as he is commanded [to fulfill them] or, even, which withholds him from fulfilling one of its obligations or one of its *sunna*s, there is no ambiguity about that: it is prohibited to consume such a thing. As opium plunges one into the state of vice which has been mentioned, what else will you then ask for as proof that it is prohibited?

In his *Commentary* on *The Orients* (*Sharḥ al-Mashāriq*), the shaykh Akmal al-Dīn [al-Bābartī][1] has said: "Among the prohibited things, there are some in which there is harmfulness to the human complexion, for example poisoned animals. Dust and clay even, to consume them is prohibited because of their harmfulness to the complexion. There are also prohibited things in which there is harmfulness to one of the attributes of [man]. Eating pork meat, for example, harms self-respect (*ghīra*); drinking wine harms being reasonable and behaving in the most correct manner concerning what is not proper; usury increases cupidity."[2]

Now that you have learned this, know that all the reasons to prohibit something which the shaykh Akmal mentioned are also found in opium, and even more [reasons]!

[Opium] is indeed harmful to man's complexion and his body, as observed and well known. [The opium eater] continuously exposes himself to perdition because, when he does not find opium one single day, he dies.

Moreover, it harms one of his attributes, i.e. good morality (*ḥusn al-khuluq*). Indeed, [the opium eater] is of bad morality. It is never possible to have a good relationship with him and he is unable to keep one single day in the company of anybody with love and friendship. Furthermore, he is unable to honour the rights of his brothers in Islam, nor the rights of relatives, neighbours, children, and he gets angry quickly. Most of the time, he is not able to learn anything, nor to read the Book. Also, because he is drowsy, he pays little attention to what is said in the councils devoted to knowledge and pious exhortation (*majlis al-'ilm wa l-wa'ẓ*). He thus remains continually ignorant.

1 Akmal al-Dīn Muḥammad b. Maḥmūd al-Bābartī al-Ḥanafī (d. in Cairo, 786/1384); see Kātib Çelebi, *Keşf*, vol. ii, col. 1688; A. Aytekin, *İA*, art. *Bābertī*. *Tuḥfat al-abrār fī sharḥ Mashāriq al-anwār* is the commentary, by Akmal al-Dīn al-Bābartī, of *Mashāriq al-anwār al-nabawiyya min Ṣiḥāḥ al-akhbār al-muṣṭafawiyya* of the imām Raḍī al-Dīn Ḥasan b. Muḥammad al-Ṣaghānī (d. in Baghdād, 650/1252); see Kātib Çelebi, *Keşf*, vol. ii, col. 1688; R. Baalbaki, *EI2*, art. *al-Ṣaghānī*; C. Brockelmann, *GAL*, *Suppl.*, vol. i, pp. 613–614.

2 The text adds "End of quote" (*intahā kalāmu-hu*).

Furthermore, [opium] weakens the intelligence. [The addict] is thus of weak intelligence and comprehension.

All this is harmful for the existence of man and a perfect life in this world. To sum up, the opium addict is transformed inwardly even if, outwardly, he has the form of a human. Some of the ulema counted the harms of wine to the body of man, to his intelligence and to his complexion, as well as the harms of opium, and they found that the harms of opium are forty times more grave.

Persians smoking opium[1]

We take refuge with God Most high against such a disgrace!

As for coffee, which has spread in our time in [all] countries, there is no reason (*wajh*) to prohibit it. [To drink] a lot of it does not make one drunk. It harms neither the complexion of man nor his body, nor any of his attributes, nor his intelligence and comprehension. It does not withhold one from fulfilling the injunctions and obligations [of the religion] but, rather, gives the strength to [fulfill] them. There is no [scriptural] text relating to it that would prove that it is prohibited. Amongst the prohibited [substances], there is nothing similar to it to which it could be linked by analogy (*qīsa ʻalā*) [so as to be declared

[1] From an Iranian drawing (Tehran, early 20th c. Private collection).

prohibited]. As for drinking it as a form of entertainment (*lahw*) and with music (*ṭarab*), in the manner of perverts (*fāsiq*), it is prohibited, as we said about concentrated grape juice (*muthallath*).[1] To sum up, only an ignorant or a fanatic (*muta'aṣṣib*) would go for prohibiting it."

* * *

THE first part of the **M** text on opium and coffee, that concerning opium, can also be found in MS. Istanbul, *Hafid Efendi 453*, ff. 85r, l. 8–86r, l. 4 (**H**), where it is explicitly related to the *Tabyīn al-maḥārim*.

The collation of the manuscripts **M** and **H** reveals the following variants and corrections:

M	**H**
P. 113, l. 1, faṣl... –> l. 2, ...ḥarām	Bism Allāh al-raḥmān al-rahīm wa bi-hi. Qāla 'alay-hi al-salām: "Kull muskir ḥarām". *Au nom de Dieu, le Clément, le Miséricordieux. [Le Prophète] a dit – sur lui la paix ! : « Tout ce qui enivre est interdit. » Quant à*
L. 3, Muḥammad	+ raḥima-hu Allāh. *Muḥammad – Dieu lui fasse miséricorde ! –*
qāla	wa qāla
L. 5, li-anna-hu	li-anna l-afyūn. *étant donné que l'opium est*
L. 7, wa l-badan	—. *l'intelligence et ne rend*
L. 9, mushāhada	mushāhad
L. 10, kathīr^{an}	+ wa lā yadrī kam yuṣallī wa yaghfulu 'an ḥāl imāmi-hi kathīr^{an} li-anna ṣāḥiba-hu fī l-nu'ās dā'im^{an} illā zamān^{an}. *beaucoup. Ils ne savent pas combien de prières accomplir et ils ne prêtent pas beaucoup d'attention à ce que leur imām fait, étant donné que l'opiomane est continuellement en train de sommeiller, sauf pour peu de temps.*
L. 11, ba'ḍ	+ min
wa qāla	anna-hu qāla
ṣallaynā	+ ṣalāt

1 *Muthallath* is the weakest of the four kinds of inebriating drinks made from grapes; see Y. Michot, *Opium*, p. 106, n. 1.

P. 112, l. 1, nāma huwa	—
L. 2, fa-baqiya	baqiya
L. 4, fa-wajadnā-hu	wa wajadnā-hu
P. 111, l. 4, ma'mūra	ma'mūr wa
L. 5, zamān	zamānu-nā
Ḥanīfa	+ raḥima-hu Allāh. *Ḥanīfa – Dieu lui fasse miséricorde ! –*
L. 6, min	'an
L. 14, shay' yuṭlabu li-yadulla	taṭlubu yadullu
P. 110, l. 1, al-dīn	+ raḥima-hu Allāh. *al-Dīn – Dieu lui fasse miséricorde ! –*
L. 2, al-masmūn	al-masmūma
L. 6, fa-yaṣīru	—
L. 8, fa-idh^{an} 'arafta	fa-idhā 'arafta hādhā fa-i'lam. *Ceci étant connu, sache que tout*
L. 9, mawjūda	mawjūd
P. 109, l. 6, al-'aql	+ fa-yakūnu khafīf al-'aql. *intelligence faible: il est d'une intelligence et d'un entendement légers.*
L. 9, mizāji-hi	+ ḍarar al-afyūn. *complexion, ainsi que les aspects nocifs de l'opium,*
fa-wajadū	fa-wajada
L. 11, al-khidhlān	+ nuqila min *Tabyīn al-maḥārim* fī bāb al-khamr wa l-maysir. *Copié de* L'exposé des choses interdites, *Chapitre du vin et des jeux de hasard.*

[1]

[1] Arab smoking. Drawing by P. Coste, Cairo, 1822 (Marseille, Bibliothèque Municipale, MS. 1307, f. 26c); see D. Jacobi, *Coste*, p. 196.

[1]

Bibliography

'Abd al-Nāfi' (*fl.* beginning of 11th/17th. c.), *Risāla takhlīṣ al-insān 'an ẓulumāt al-dukhān*, in F. Klein-Franke, *Smoking*, pp. 172–183. [*Takhlīṣ*].

Abū Dā'ūd (d. 275/889), *al-Sunan*, ed. 'Abd al-Ḥamīd, 4 vols (Beirut: Dār Iḥyā' al-Sunnat al-Nabawiyya, n.d.). [*Sunan*].

Amāsī (al-), Yūsuf Sinān al-Dīn (d. 986/1578), *Tabyīn al-maḥārim*, MS. Ankara, Milli Kütüphane, *Nevşehir Damad İbrahim Paşa İl Halk Kütüphanesi*, 50 Damad 253, ff. 31r–32r. [*Tabyīn*].

Andrews, W. G. & Kalpaklı, M., *The Age of Beloveds. Love and the Beloved in Early-Modern Ottoman and European Culture and Society* (Durham–London: Duke University Press, 2005). [*Age*].

Aqḥiṣārī (al-), Aḥmad b. Muḥammad al-Rūmī (d. 1041/1631 or 1043/1634), *Majālis al-abrār wa masālik al-akhyār*, MS. *Michot 0402*. [*Majālis*].

See also the incomplete editions and Urdu translations of S. B. al-Shikārpūrī, *Khazīna*, and 'A. W. al-Madrāsī, *Maṭāriḥ*, as well as the Turkish version of *Councils XVII*, *XVIII*, *LVII* & *LVIII* in M. B. Eryarsoy & M. el-Humeyyis, *Risaleleri*.

–, *Sharḥ* al-Durr al-yatīm *fī l-tajwīd li-l-Birgivī*, MS. Istanbul, *Harput 429*, ff. 1v–28r. [*Sharḥ*].

–, *Radd al-qabriyya*, MS. *Michot 0801*, ff. 1v–20r. [*Qabriyya*].

–, *Risāla fī ḥurmat al-raqṣ wa l-dawarān*, MS. Istanbul, *Harput 429*, ff. 65r–72r. [*Raqṣ*].

–, *Risāleh*, MS. *Michot 0802*, ff. 65v–85r. [*Risāleh*].

[1] Drawing by M. Jaspar, in L. Paquot-Pierret, *Vengeance*, p. 19.

Azharī (al-), Karīm al-Dīn Ḥusayn (*fl.* end of 11th/17th. c.), *Risāla fī ḥukm shurb al-dukhān*, in F. Klein-Franke, *Smoking*, pp. 184–192. [*Ḥukm*].

Bakla, E., *Tophane lüleciliği. Osmanlı'nın tasarımdaki yaratıcılığı ve yaşam keyfi* (Istanbul: Antik A.Ş. Kültür Yayınları, 2007). [*Tophane*].

Berger, L., *Ein Herz wie ein trockener Schwamm. Laqānīs und Nābulusīs Schriften über den Tabakrauch*, in *Der Islam*, 78 (2001), pp. 249–293. [*Hertz*].

Billings, E. R., *Tobacco: its History, Varieties, Culture, Manufacture and Commerce, with an Account of its Various Modes of Use, from its First Discovery until Now* (Hartford: American Publishing Company, 1875). [*Tobacco*].

Birnbaum, E., *Vice Triumphant: The Spread of Coffee and Tobacco in Turkey*, in *Durham University Journal* (Dec. 1956), pp. 21–27. [*Vice*].

Bobovius, Albertus (d. 1675?), *Topkapi. Relation du sérail du Grand Seigneur*. Édition présentée et annotée par A. Berthier et S. Yerasimos (Arles: Actes Sud, "Sindbad. La Bibliothèque turque", 1999). [*Topkapi*].

Brockelmann, C., *Geschichte der Arabischen Litteratur* (Leiden: E. J. Brill, vol. i, 1943; vol. II, 1949; *Supplement*, vol. I, 1937; vol. ii, 1938; vol. iii, 1942). – Reprint: Leiden: E. J. Brill, 1996. [*GAL*].

Brown, J. P., *The Dervishes; or, Oriental Spiritualism* (London: Trübner & Co., 1868). [*Dervishes*].

Bukhārī (al-; d. 256/870), *al-Ṣaḥīḥ*, 9 vols (Bulaq: al-Maṭba'at al-kubrā l-amīriyya, 1311–1313/[1893–1895]). [*Ṣaḥīḥ*].

Çavuşoğlu, S., *The Kadizadeli Movement: An Attempt of Şeri' at-minded Reform in the Ottoman Empire* (Ph.D. diss., Princeton University, 1990). [*Movement*].

Chute, Anthony (d. 1595?), *Tabacco* (London: William Barlow, 1595). [*Tabacco*].

Contes des Mille et Une Nuits. Le marchand de Bagdad, Le cheval enchanté et autres contes (Paris: Larousse, "Les Livres Bleus", 1928). [*Contes*].

Dārimī (al-), Abū Muḥammad 'Abd Allāh (d. 255/869), *al-Sunan*, 2 vols (Cairo: Dār al-Fikr, 1398/1978). – Anastatic reprint: Beirut, Dār al-Fikr, n.d. [*Sunan*].

De Bruyn, C., *Voyages de Corneille le Bruyn au Levant, C'est-à-dire, dans les Principaux endroits de l'Asie Mineure, Dans les Isles de Chio, Rhodes, Chypre, &c. De même que dans les plus considérables Villes d'Egypte, Syrie, & Terre Sainte*..., 2 vols (The Hague: P. Gosse & J. Neaulme, 1732). [*Voyages*].

De Jong, F. & Radtke, B. (eds), *Islamic Mysticism Contested: Thirteen Centuries of Controversies and Polemics* (Leiden: Brill, "Islamic History and Civilization. Studies and Texts, 29", 1999). [*Mysticism*].

Düzdağ, M. E., *Şeyhülislām Ebussu'ūd Efendi'nin fetvalarına göre Kanunī devrinde Osmanlı hayatı – Fetāvā-yı Ebussu'ūd Efendi* (Istanbul: Ş ūle Yayınları, 1998). [*Hayatı*].

Encyclopaedia of Islam. New edition: Vol. i, Leiden: E. J. Brill – Paris: Maisonneuve, M. Besson, 1960; vols ii–xii, Suppl., Leiden: E. J. Brill – Paris: Maisonneuve & Larose, 1965-2007. [*EI2*].

Eryarsoy, M. B. & el-Humeyyis, M, *Ahmed er-Rūmī el-Hanefī Akāid Risaleleri. Kabirler, Bid'atler ve Ölümü Hatırlama* (Istanbul: Guraba, 1423/ 2002). [*Risaleleri*].

Fishbein, M., *The Victory of Islam. Muḥammad at Medina (A.D. 626–630/A.H. 5–8)*. Translated and annotated. Vol. viii of: *The History of al-Ṭabarī (Ta'rīkh al-rusul wa'l-mulūk)*. Edited by E. Yar-Shater, 38 vols (Albany: State University of New York Press, "Bibliotheca Persica", 1985–1989). [*Conquest*].

Gaborieau, Marc, *A Nineteenth-Century Indian 'Wahhabi' Tract Against the Cult of Muslim Saints*: Al-Balāgh al-Mubīn, in *Muslim Shrines in India. Their Character, History and Significance*, edited by Christian W. Troll (Delhi: Oxford University Press, "Islam in India: Studies and Commentaries IV", 1992), pp. 198–239. [*Tract*].

–, *Criticizing the Sufis: The Debate in Early-Nineteenth Century India*, in F. de Jong & B. Radtke (eds), *Mysticism*, pp. 452–467. [*Criticizing*].

Gacek, A., *The Arabic Manuscript Tradition. A Glossary of Technical Terms & Bibliography. Supplement* (Leiden–Boston: Brill, 2008). [*Supplement*].

Ghazālī (al-), Abū Ḥāmid (d. 505/1111), *Iḥyā' 'ulūm al-dīn*, 4 vols (Cairo: 'Īsā l-Bābī l-Ḥalabī, 1377/1957). [*Iḥyā'*].
See also L. Zolondek, *Ādāb*.

Grehan, J., *Smoking and "Early Modern" Sociability: The Great Tobacco Debate in the Ottoman Middle East (Seventeenth to Eighteenth Centuries)*, in *American Historical Review* (Dec. 2006), pp. 1352–1377. [*Smoking*].

Guer, J. A., *Mœurs et Usages des Turcs, leur Religion, leur Gouvernement civil, militaire et politique, Avec un Abrégé de l'Histoire Ottomane*, 2 vols (Paris: Merigot & Piget, 1747). [*Mœurs*].

Hallaq, W. B., *Was the Gate of* Ijtihād *Closed?*, in *International Journal of Middle East Studies*, 16/1 (1984), pp. 3-41. [*Gate*].

Hattox, R. S., *Coffee and Coffeehouses. The Origins of a Social Beverage in the Medieval Near East* (Seattle–London: University of Washington Press, 1996). [*Coffee*].

Haythamī (al-), Nūr al-Dīn 'Alī (d. 807/1404), *Majma' al-zawā'id wa manba' al-fawā'id*, 10 vols (Cairo: Maktabat al-Qudsī, 1352[/1933]–1353[/1934]). [*Majma'*].

Ibn Ḥanbal (d. 241/855), *al-Musnad*, 6 vols (Cairo: al-Bābī l-Ḥalabī, 1313/ [1896]). – Anastatic reprint: Beirut: al-Maktab al-islāmī, 1403/1983. [*Musnad*].

Ibn Kathīr (d. 774/1373), *Tafsīr al-Qur'ān al-'aẓīm*, 4 vols (Beirut: Dār al-Jayl, 1410/1990). [*Tafsīr*].

Ibn Māja (d. 273/887), *al-Sunan*, ed. M. F. 'Abd al-Bāqī, 2 vols (Cairo: 1373/ 1954). – Anastatic reprint: Beirut: Dār al-Fikr, n.d. [*Sunan*].

Ibn Sīnā (d. 428/1037), *al-Qānūn fī l-ṭibb*, ed. E. al-Qish & 'A. Zay'ūr, 4 vols (Beirut: Mu'assasat 'Izz al-Dīn li-l-Ṭibā'a wa l-Nashr, 1413/1993). [*Qānūn*].

Ibn Taymiyya (d. 728/1328), *Majmū' al-fatāwā*, ed. 'A. R. b. M. Ibn Qāsim, 37 vols (Rabat: Maktabat al-Ma'ārif, 1401/1981). [*MF*].

İnalcık, H. & Renda, G. (eds), *Ottoman Civilization*, 2 vols (Ankara: Ministry of Turism and Culture, 2004). [*Civilization*].

İslām Ansiklopedisi, 35 vols (Istanbul: Türkiye Diyanet Vakfı, 1988–). [*İA*].

Jacobi, D. (ed.), *Pascal Coste. Toutes les Égypte* (Marseille: Bibliothèque Municipale de Marseille – Éditions Parenthèses, 1998). [*Coste*].

Karmī (al-), Mar'ī b. Yūsuf (d. 1033/1623–4), *Taḥqīq al-burhān fī sha'n al-dukhān alladhī yashrabu-hu l-nās al-ān*, ed. A. 'U. M. b. Ḥ. Āl Salmān (Beirut: Dār Ibn Ḥazm: 1421/2000). [*Taḥqīq*].

Kātib Çelebi (d. 1067/1657), *Keşf-el-Zunun*, ed. Ş. Yaltkaya – K. R. Bilge, 2 vols (Istanbul: Maarif Matbaası, 1941–1943). [*Keşf*].

–, *Mīzānü'l-Hak fī İhtiyāri'l-Ehakk. İslam'da Tenkit ve Tartışma Usūlü*, ed. S. Uludağ & M. Kara (Istanbul: Marifet Yayınları, 2001). [*Mīzān*].
See the translation by G. L. Lewis, *Balance*.

Kattānī (al-), Muḥammad b. Ja'far (d. 1927), *I'lān al-ḥujja wa iqāmat al-burhān 'alā mā 'amma wa fashā min isti'māl 'ushbat al-dukhān* (Damascus: 1990). [*I'lān*].

Keene, H. G., *An Oriental Biographical Dictionary* (London: W. H. Allen & Co., 1894). [*Dictionary*].

Klein-Franke, F., *No Smoking in Paradise: The Habit of Tobacco Smoking Judged by Muslim Law*, in *Le Muséon*, 106 (1993), pp. 155–192. [*Smoking*].

Laqānī (al-), Ibrāhīm (d. 1041/1631), *Kitāb naṣīḥat al-ikhwān bi-ijtināb al-dukhān*, ed. A. M. Āl Maḥmūd (Bahrain: Bahrain University, Faculty of Letters, 1413/1993). On internet: *staff.uob.bh/files/490044336_files/NEEHATALKAL.doc*. [*Naṣīḥa*].

Lewis, B., *Istanbul and the Civilization of the Ottoman Empire* (Norman: University of Oklahoma Press, 1963). [*Istanbul*].

Lewis, G. L., *The Balance of Truth by Kātib Chelebi*. Translated with an Introduction and Notes (London: George Allen and Unwin, "Ethical and Religious Classics of East and West", 1957). [*Balance*].

Lozano, I., *Solaz del espíritu en el hachís y el vino y otros textos árabes sobre drogas (Con fragmentos de P. Alpino y A. Russell)*. Introducción, traducción y notas (Granada: Editorial Universidad de Granada, 1998). [*Solaz*].

Madrāsī (al-), 'Abd al-Walī, *Maṭāriḥ al-anẓār, tarjama Majālis al-abrār* (Lucknow: Maṭba'at al-Āsī l-Madrāsī, 1321[/1903]). [*Maṭāriḥ*].

Mālik b. Anas (d. 179/796), *al-Muwaṭṭa', ma'a sharḥ al-'allāma 'Abd al-Ḥayy al-Liknawī*, ed. T. D. al-Nadwī, 3 vols (Muzaffarpur: al-Jāmi'at al-islāmiyya, 1419/1999). [*Muwaṭṭa'*].

Melling, A. I., *Voyage pittoresque de Constantinople et des rives du Bosphore* (Paris: M. M. Treuttel & Würtz, 1819). [*Voyage*].

Michot, Y., *Ibn Taymiyya. Le haschich et l'extase*. Textes traduits de l'arabe, présentés et annotés (Beirut: Albouraq, "Fetwas d'Ibn Taymiyya, 3", 1422/2001). [*Haschich*].

–, *Muslims under Non-Muslim Rule. Ibn Taymiyya on fleeing from sin, kinds of emigration, the status of Mardin (domain of peace/war, domain composite), the conditions for challenging power*. Texts translated, annotated and presented in relation to six modern readings of the Mardin fatwā. Foreword by J. Piscatori (Oxford–London: Interface Publications, 2006). [*Muslims*].

–, *L'opium et le café*. Édition et traduction d'un texte arabe anonyme, précédées d'une première exploration de l'opiophagie ottomane et accompagnées d'une anthologie (Paris–Beirut: Albouraq, 1429/2008). [*Opium*].

Morier, J., *The Adventures of Hajji Baba of Ispahan*. Illustrated by C. Leroy Baldridge (New York: Random House, 1937). [*Adventures*].

Muderrisoğlu, M. E., *Akhisarlı Türk Büyükleri ve Eserleri* (Izmir: Piyasa Matbaası, 1956). [*Akhisarlı*].

Muḥibbī (al-), Muḥammad Amīn b. Faḍl Allāh (d. 1111/1699), *Khulāṣat al-athar fī a'yān al-qarn al-ḥādī 'ashar*, 4 vols (Cairo: al-Maṭba'at al-Wahbiyya, 1284[/1868]). [*Khulāṣa*].

Muslim (d. 261/875), *Al-Jāmi' al-ṣaḥīḥ*, 8 vols (Constantinople, 1334/[1916]). – Anastatic reprint: Beirut: al-Maktab al-tijārī li-l-ṭibā'a wa l-nashr wa l-tawzī', n.d. [*Ṣaḥīḥ*].

Nābulusī (al-), 'Abd al-Ghanī (d. 1143/1731), *Risāla fī ibāḥat al-dukhān*, ed. A. M. Dahmān (Damascus: Maṭba'at al-Iṣlāḥ, 1343[/1924]). [*Ibāḥa*].

Nasā'ī (al-; d. 303/915), *al-Sunan*, 8 vols (Beirut: Dār al-Kutub al-'Ilmiyya, n.d. [*Sunan*].

Ocak, A. Y., *Oppositions au soufisme dans l'empire ottoman aux quinzième et seizième siècles*, in F. de Jong & B. Radtke (eds), *Mysticism*, pp. 603–613. [*Oppositions*].

–, *Religious Sciences and the Ulema*, in H. İnalcık & G. Renda (eds), *Civilization*, pp. 243–365.

Özel, A., *Hanefi Fıkıh Alimleri* (Ankara: Türkiye Diyanet Vakfı, "Kaynak Eserler Serisi, 1", 2006). [*Alimleri*].

Paquot-Pierret, L., *La vengeance de Bakhtiyar*. Illustrations de M. Jaspar (Brussels: Office de Publicité, 1939). [*Vengeance*].

Peters, R., *The Battered Dervishes of Bab Zuwayla. A Religious Riot in Eighteenth-Century Cairo*, in Levtzion, N. & Voll, J. O. (eds), *Eighteenth-Century Renewal and Reform in Islam* (Syracuse: Syracuse University Press, 1987). [*Dervishes*].

Pinchon, J. P., *Becassine chez les Turcs*. Texte de Caumery (Paris: Gautier-Languereau, 1919). [*Becassine*].

Rāzī (al-), Fakhr al-Dīn (d. 606/1209), *al-Tafsīr al-kabīr*, 32 vols (Cairo: al-Maṭba'at al-Bahiyya, 1357/1938). [*Tafsīr*].

Rosenthal, F., *The Herb. Hashish versus Medieval Muslim Society* (Leiden: E. J. Brill, 1971). [*Herb*].

Saraçgıl, A., *Generi voluttuari e ragion di stato. Politiche repressive del consumo di vino, caffè e tabacco nell' impero ottomano nei secc. XVI e XVII*, in *Turcica*, 28 (1996), pp. 163–194. [*Generi*].

Shikārpūrī (al-), Subḥān Bakhsh, *Khazīnat al-asrār, tarjama Majālis al-abrār* (Delhi: Maṭba' Muṣṭafā'ī, 1283[/1866]). [*Khazīna*].

Ṭabarī, Ibn Jarīr (d. 310/922), *Ta'rīkh al-umam wa l-mulūk*, 13 vols (Cairo: al-Maṭba'at al-Ḥusayniyya, 1323[/1905]). [*Ta'rīkh*].

See also M. Fishbein, *Victory*.

Taeschner, F., *Alt-Stambuler Hof-und Volksleben. Ein Türkisches Miniaturenalbum aus dem 17. Jahrhundert*. I. Tafelband (Hanovre, 1925). – Anastatic reprint: Osnabrück: Biblio Verlag, 1978. [*Volksleben*].

Vereschaguine, B., *Voyage dans l'Asie centrale*, in *Le Tour du monde*, vol. xxv (Paris: 1873), pp. 193–272. [*Voyage*].

Yāqūt (d. 626/1229), *Mu'jam al-buldān*, ed. F. 'A. 'A. al-Jundī, 7 vols (Beirut: Dār al-Kutub al-'Ilmiyya, 1410/1990). [*Mu'jam*].

Zilfi, M. C., *The Kadizadelis: Discordant Revivalism in the Seventeenth Century Istanbul*, in *Journal of Near Eastern Studies*, 45 (1986), pp. 251–269. [*Kadizadelis*].

–, *The Politics of Piety: the Ottoman Ulema in the Postclassical Age* (*1600–1800*) (Minneapolis: Bibliotheca Islamica, "Studies in Middle Eastern History, 8", 1988). [*Politics*].

Ziriklī (al-), Kh. D., *al-A'lām. Qāmūs tarājim li-ashhar al-rijāl wa l-nisā' min al-'Arab wa l-musta'rabīn wa l-mustashriqīn*, 8 vols (Beirut: Dār al-'Ilm li-l-Malāyīn, 1990). [*A'lām*].

Zolondek, L., *Book XX of al-Ghazālī's* Iḥyā' 'Ulūm al-Dīn. Translated from the Arabic (Leiden: Brill, 1963). [*Ādāb*].

Indexes

Page numbers shown in **bold** indicate occurrences within passages of al-Aqḥiṣārī' writings.

QUR'ĀNIC VERSES

ḤADĪTHS OF THE PROPHET

GEOGRAPHICAL TERMS

PERSONS, GROUPS, DOCTRINES

KEYWORDS AND CONCEPTS

TRANSCRIBED WORDS